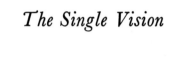

The Single Vision

The Single Vision

The Alienation of
American Intellectuals

Ernest Earnest

New York · New York University Press
London · University of London Press Ltd
1970

ACKNOWLEDGMENTS

Excerpts from Sinclair Lewis' *Dodsworth* © 1929, E. E. Cummings' *Portraits III* © 1954, Lewis Mumford's *Technics and Civilization* © 1934, and John Crowe Ransom's *God without Thunder* © 1930 by Harcourt, Brace & World. Reprinted with permission.

Excerpt from Dorothy Parker's "Neither Bloody nor Bowed" from *The Portable Dorothy Parker* © 1926 by Viking Press, renewed by Dorothy Parker in 1954. Reprinted with permission of The Viking Press, Inc.

Excerpts from Edgar Lee Masters' *Spoon River Anthology* © 1915 by The Macmillan Co. Reprinted with permission.

Excerpts from Stuart Sherman's *Points of View* © 1924 by Charles Scribner's Sons. Reprinted with permission.

May God us keep
From single vision . . .

William Blake

My grateful acknowledgments are due to Dean George
W. Johnson and Professor Richard S. Kennedy of Temple
University, and to Professor Oscar Cargill of New York
University, all of whom read portions of my manuscript and
offered helpful criticism. My wife Maude gave me suggestions
and much editorial assistance. My thanks also to Temple
University for a grant-in-aid which provided for secretarial
expenses.

Contents

Introduction

To a remarkable degree American writers between 1910 and 1930 dominated the national literary scene for another thirty years. It seems clear that no American novelist who first appeared after 1930 has had a stature comparable to that of Dreiser, Hemingway, Fitzgerald, Faulkner, or Dos Passos; no dramatist has come close to O'Neill, no poet to Eliot, Frost, or Wallace Stevens. This is not to say that these men did not do important work after the twenties, but all of them had appeared on the literary scene before 1930. It is also safe to say that no novelist since Sinclair Lewis has had a comparable impact on our society, not only in giving the Main Streets and Babbitts a local habitation and a name but in forcing the United States to reexamine its code of values. There are far better novelists than Lewis, but not since Harriet Beecher Stowe had there been so influential a one.

A similar situation exists in criticism. H. L. Mencken was, as will appear, wrong in his estimates of a variety of writers, and much of his social criticism now is obsolete. Yet for about a decade he dominated the critical scene almost like a Samuel Johnson. A more lasting critical influence has been that of T. S. Eliot beginning with *The Sacred Wood* (1920). And of course before Eliot there was Pound whose critical blasts and whose discoveries of new talent set the stage for modern poetry. Along with Pound and Eliot there were Randolph Bourne and the early Van Wyck Brooks who helped create the climate for the literature of the 1920s, indeed for the next thirty years. Edmund Wilson, who began critical writing in the twenties, continued to be a major figure in the sixties. This is not to belittle the importance of such editors as Margaret Anderson, Harriet Monroe, and Robert McAlmon who were among the first to publish the work of Pound, Lindsay, Eliot, Hart Crane, Wallace Stevens, William Carlos Williams, Joyce, Sherwood Anderson, and Hemingway.

Of course these critics and editors did not all move in the same direction. Brooks, Bourne, and Mencken were much concerned with the inhibiting weight of the Puritan heritage; Pound and Eliot with the loss of the European heritage. More than the others Pound and Eliot were concerned with technique. But all tended to see twentieth-century America as a cultural wasteland. In this view they were joined by a cloud of witnesses: critics, novelists, poets.

Along with this dim view of American culture there was a disillusion with democracy—on the one hand painted as a sham, on the other as the enemy of culture. A generation of muckrakers had exposed the corruption of government from city hall to Washington, D. C. The betrayal of the Progressive movement by Woodrow Wilson had alienated most intellectuals from politics. In fact under

Wilson's attorney-general Palmer and in the Harding-Coolidge era, intellectual dissent tended to be equated with treason.

Two key books greatly influenced the intellectuals of the 1920s: *The Education of Henry Adams* (1918) and Charles Beard's *An Economic Interpretation of the Constitution of the United States* (1913). Adams portrayed the alienation of the intellectual, or even the honest man, from national government; Beard represented the Constitution as the result of conspiracy by the wealthy against disfranchised farmers and workingmen. The validity of this view will be discussed later, but a survey in 1935 showed that 37 out of 42 college texts had adopted the Beard thesis.[1] Many of the critics during the 1920s accepted Beard's view as an article of faith.

The foregoing brief outline suggests some of the topics to be considered in this study of what has been called the second American literary renaissance. The first is of course that represented by Poe, Emerson, Thoreau, Hawthorne, Melville, and Whitman. For the purpose of this study the era of the second renaissance lies somewhere between 1910 and 1930. It is not so neat a category as "the Twenties," that period between the end of World War I and the great depression. In that decade poetry, the novel, drama, and literary criticism clearly embodied a group of related themes: the revolt against puritanism; disillusion with the values of Main Street and Zenith; a cynicism about professed American ideals, especially those of Protestantism and democracy; and on the positive side a search for new literary forms and models, especially those of Continental Europe as opposed to traditional English models. It was a period of intensive literary discussion and criticism, one such as Wordsworth experienced when he dragged

> . . . all precepts, judgments, maxims, creeds
> Like culprits to the bar; calling the mind
> Suspiciously, to establish in plain day
> Her titles and her honours. . . .[2]

However, every one of these themes and tendencies had appeared in American literature before the war. Malcolm Cowley states, "The real war had been fought in the decade before 1920, when almost every writer was a recruit to the army against gentility, and when older writers like Dreiser and Robinson were being rescued from neglect and praised as leaders." [3]

It might even be argued that much of the real war had been fought in the 1890s with the demand by Howells and Garland for realism; and in the novels of Harold Frederic, Henry B. Fuller, Stephen Crane, and Frank Norris. Howells' squeamishness about sex in literature was countered by writers demanding what James called "the larger latitude." Nor was the pre-renaissance period so barren as the younger iconoclasts liked to think. The decade 1895 to 1905 saw the appearance of a great many novels of lasting merit, among them Harold Frederic's *The Damnation of Theron Ware;* Henry B. Fuller's *The Cliff Dwellers;* Stephen Crane's *The Red Badge of Courage;* William Dean Howells' *A Hazard of New Fortunes;* Frank Norris' *Mac Teague* and *The Octopus;* S. Weir Mitchell's *Constance Trescott;* Theodore Dreiser's *Sister Carrie;* Edith Wharton's *The House of Mirth;* Henry James' *The Ambassadors, The Wings of the Dove,* and *The Golden Bowl.* If it be objected that these last were by an expatriate, it must be remembered that a number of landmarks of the 1920s were also by expatriated Americans, for instance *The Waste Land, The Sun Also Rises,* and *A Farewell to Arms*. In fact *Babbitt* and *The Great Gatsby* were written in Europe.

The 1890s and early 1900s also produced the literary criticism of James Gibbon Huneker of Philadelphia—a city which Mencken with some justice at the time called "that depressing intellectual slum." Huneker introduced Americans to the modern European scene. As Oscar Cargill puts it:

> Name almost any important name in art, music, or literature in Scandinavia, Germany, France, or England in the latter half of the nineteenth century, and it is a safe bet that James Gibbon Huneker was the first to write intelligently upon that artist in America. He was the most important early crusader here for Ibsen, Shaw, Sudermann, Hauptmann, Huysmans, Stendhal, Maeterlinck, Richard Strauss, Anatole France, Barrés, Stirner and Nietzsche.[4]

Mencken stated that Huneker "was the first to give a hand to Frank Norris, Theodore Dreiser, Stephen Crane, and H. B. Fuller." [5] Certainly many of the literary enthusiasms of critics between 1915 and 1930 are far more outdated than those of Huneker a generation earlier.

All this is to suggest that our second literary renaissance was not the sudden flowering in a desert which it has so often been considered, nor was it primarily the consequence of World War I. That is not to say that the War had no influence on literature, but that its influence has probably been exaggerated.

However the exact dating of the second renaissance is less important than the question of its quality. What were its lasting achievements, and wherein did it fail?

The first part of the question has been considered in various studies, notably in Alfred Kazin's *On Native Grounds* and Frederick Hoffman's *The Twenties*. Other valuable discussions are Malcolm Cowley's *After the Genteel Tradition* and Edmund Wilson's *The Shores of Light*. All of these deal with the limitations of various writers as well as with their strengths. But it seems safe to say that none of these critics deals fully with the limitations of the period as a whole. It is this problem to which the present study is devoted.

My thesis is that despite the considerable achievements of this renaissance, its dominance of American literature has not been entirely wholesome: certain limitations of vision shared by writers between 1910 and 1930 produced distortions in our literature for a long time. Perhaps the greatest myopia was in the field of political vision, but that is a matter for more detailed examination. In any event, it is hardly too much to say that the second American renaissance was a watershed for the intellectuals. Before it many writers had been critical of our society, but few of them denied its fundamental values; however, during the period under consideration critics, historians, poets and novelists raised questions about these values or denied them entirely. My theory is that in their alienation from American society they created an intellectual climate which endures to this day.

As the foregoing suggests, the present study is chiefly concerned with the ideas of the writers during the period rather than with their artistic achievement. It is essentially written from the point of view of a devil's advocate. Others have ably presented the arguments for beatification.

The Single Vision

1.

The Distorting Rear-View Mirror

"Ignorance, pure ignorance, madam," said Dr. Johnson in explanation of a mistake a lady had pointed out in his dictionary. The same might be said of much of the writing between 1910 and 1930 on nineteenth-century American art and literature.

Henry James had set the pattern. Certainly his view of America's cultural past became a cliché with writers during the first three decades of this century. This view, expressed most fully in his life of Hawthorne (1879), was that American life was too thin to nurture the writer. Elsewhere James stated that Thoreau "is worse than provincial, he is parochial." James could not know, of course, that Thoreau would be one of the seminal thinkers in twentieth-century life and thought, but he should have known that Ruskin and William Morris were indebted to Thoreau. Even a careful reading of *Civil Disobedience* should have told him that the writer was dealing with a theme as universal as the *Antigone* of Sophocles. Certainly

Walden challenged the whole premises of industrial society; it had even more to say to Victorian England than to a still predominantly rural America.

A key figure to the myth of the baleful effect of America on the artist was Washington Allston. Henry James in his *Life and Letters of William Wetmore Story* printed a letter of 1855 in which the sculptor said:

> Allston starved spiritually in Cambridgeport. There was nothing congenial without and he turned his powers inward and drained his memory dry. . . . I know no more melancholy sight than he was, so rich and beautiful a nature . . . stunted on the scant soil and withered by the cold winds of that fearful Cambridgeport.[1]

This view was echoed as late as 1957 by Van Wyck Brooks who spoke of "the classic case, so often repeated in America, of Washington Allston. It exemplified all the old warnings of so many critics about the fate of the artist in our undeveloped country." The "many critics" were of course those of the period under discussion—including Brooks.

However, Allston himself, the friend of Coleridge and, had he stayed in England, the probable successor to West as president of the Royal Academy, wrote enthusiastically in 1827 of a Boston art exhibit: "I have seen worse in London." He was pleased with its "astonishing success with the public." The prominent English art historian, Mrs. Anna B. Jameson, who visited Boston in 1838, regarded the paintings which Allston did after his return to America as his most original and distinctive work. This opinion is shared by the modern art historian, Edgar Richardson, who in 1956 argued that Allston's landscape reveries upon nature, done after his return to America, represent the aspect of his art most appealing to modern taste.[2]

It was Brooks, who in his early critical writing, took up the Jamesian theme of the cultural poverty of America. In *The Wine of the Puritans* (1908) he started with the premise that, "American history is so unloveable." * Writing of Whistler and Sargent he stated a thesis which was to become a cliché for fifty years: "But how in the world is an artist to cultivate a racial tradition when as you and I have been trying to show, America has no tradition." [3]

Such a statement could only be written by someone ignorant of the work of Copley, Charles Willson Peale, Morse, Mount, Bingham, Eakins, and Homer—a body of painting that any informed critic would recognize instantly as American. Allied to it are the paintings and carvings of anonymous local craftsmen, and of the popular lithographs of Currier and Ives—the expression of what John A. Kouwenhoven calls "the vernacular tradition," which he has shown to be an enduring and powerful force in American architecture, machine design, art and letters.

In time Brooks became aware of his blindness to the American cultural past. Years later an exhibition at the Whitney museum of American primitives opened his eyes to an artistic tradition.

Then came the work of Constance Rourke:

---

* Brooks apparently forgot Gulliver's report of the king of Brobdingnag's view of English history:

He was perfectly astonished with the historical account I gave him of our affairs during the last century; protesting it was only a heap of conspiracies, rebellions, murders, massacres, revolutions, banishments, the very worst effects that avarice, faction, hypocrisy, perfidiousness, cruelty, rage, madness, hatred, envy, lust, malice, or ambition could produce.

Thus at a time when American writers were deeply concerned with the country and were beginning to explore its spiritual resources Constance Rourke brought together a thousand concrete evidences of the widespread folk-culture of the past.[4]

Brooks' ignorance of American folk-culture is more excusable than his misreading of literature. For instance:

One sees in Whittier, Holmes and the rest that preconception of the supreme virtues of thrift and industry, the note of shrewdness and homely comfort showing that Puritanism had not yet accustomed itself to prosperity or to allowing the unqualified value of anything not essentially and directly connected with the machinery of life.[5]

Now had Brooks read nothing but *Proem,* the first poem in Whittier's collected works, he would have found it to be a lament for the poet's inability to rival Spenser, Sidney, Marvel, and Milton; he had been hindered by the lack of poetic training, by the duties of a busy life, and by his own limitations. But such gifts as he has he will lay upon Freedom's shrine. Anyone who has read Whittier's anti-slavery poems will recognize that he tried to do just that. Idealism not thrift, self-sacrifice not shrewdness were Whittier's themes. The young Dartmouth man in *Snow Bound* will go forth as one of Freedom's young apostles to right ancient wrongs, refute "the cruel lie of caste," and plant a schoolhouse on every hill.

As for Holmes, there runs throughout *The Autocrat* his contempt for Puritan prejudices and middle-class mediocrity. The "self-made man, whittled into shape with his own jack-knife" deserves great credit but as for Holmes, *"other things being equal,* in most relations of life I prefer a man of family."

Brooks was equally obtuse about American humorists:

> But our humour is a kind which has neither past nor future, but only the moment of its flash, a humour not sprung from genial soil nor reflecting the tears and smiles of dead generations . . . it is a humour . . . of pure intelligence, so harsh that if it expressed an enduring mood it would be cynical. . . .
>
> Yes our humour has undoubtedly drifted apart and ceased to be an expression of life. And our humorists are homeless, nameless vagrants.[6]

In support of tnis last statement he complained that "They never write under their own names. Mark Twain, Artemus Ward, Josh Billings, Mr. Dooley—they have never spoken through their own lips." One pauses in awe at the thought of Mark Twain and Mr. Dooley as homeless, nameless, vagrants. As for pseudonyms, had Brooks never heard of Isaac Bickerstaff, Lemuel Gulliver, The Spectator, Waverley, George Sand, George Elliot, or Boz?

These generalizations and misconceptions by an angry young man would not now be of importance had they not taken their place among the critical clichés which were to be recited as holy writ for a generation. Some of them, like the lack of an American tradition, endured for fifty years. Brooks was still repeating the myth of Washington Allston over a hundred years after Story had started it. Brooks later admitted that when he began writing about American literature he had read little of the nineteenth-century writers. However it was his early work which helped to set the pattern for the 1910–1930 period. After 1930 he tended to become an amiable antiquarian.

Following the jejune *Wine of the Puritans* he produced the more influential *America's Coming of Age*
(1915). Here, along with Mencken and others, he developed
the theme of America's poverty-stricken literary past.
"Longfellow is to poetry . . . what the barrel-organ is
to music. . . . Emerson was imperfectly interested in
human life. . . . In spite of their frequent show of
strength and boldness, no ideas in America are really
strong or bold. . . ." [7] The book barely mentions Thoreau
and omits Melville entirely.* Only Whitman emerges as
an important force who "laid the cornerstone of a national
ideal capable in this way of releasing personality and of
retrieving for our civilization, originally deficient in the
richer pieces of human nature, and still further bled and
flattened out by the 'machine process,' the only sort of
'place in the sun' that is really worth having." But even
Whitman suffered because his large share of "the naive
pioneer nature . . . made it impossible for him to take
experience very seriously. . . . As he grew older, the sensuality of his nature led him astray in a vast satisfaction
with material facts, before which he purred like a cat by
the warm fire." [8] Obviously Brooks had not read *Democratic Vistas,* that troubled examination of American
materialism and corruption. It seems doubtful that Brooks
had even read *Drum Taps,* perhaps the most realistic war
poetry of the nineteenth century.†

* Although a biography of Melville had not yet appeared, John Macy,
in *The Spirit of American Literature,* 1908, had praised *Moby Dick.*

† Richard Aldington, speaking of *Drum Taps* wrote: "Up to then, the
killings, the maimings, the sufferings and miseries of war had been as
unreal to me as the murders in a detective story. Whitman made me see
the reality; and I believe he has the honor of being the only poet of the
19th century to tell the truth about war." *Life for Life's Sake,* N. Y., 1961,
p. 120.

Although Brooks' ideas later changed, he had already developed his confusing sentence structure interlarded with tag-ends of quotations. In his preface to the revised edition of 1934 he admitted to a "vague horror of having appeared to disparage these older worthies . . . because one finds in them today—in some of them, at least—the large mental bones and hardy sinews that indicate an important race."

The same pessimistic view prevailed in his *Letters and Leadership* (1918). "We have no American culture, no; but we have an 'American spirit,' the spirit which produced Sousa's music and Howard Chandler Christie's art and Mrs. Eddy's religion. . . ." [9] This sentence has two characteristics of much of the critical writing of the time: the use of loaded dice and the tendency to regard American tendencies as unique. The loaded-dice technique became the trademark of Mencken, who scoured the public prints for examples of the meretricious and the inane which were then represented as typical. Sinclair Lewis exploited this technique to the full in his novels. It has a place in satire, but not in a considered evaluation of art, literature, or society. The second tendency, the only-in-America theme which represents our national failings as unique, will be treated in some detail later in this book. It is loading the dice to pick Howard Chandler Christie instead of Winslow Homer, Thomas Eakins or William Glackens. As for Sousa, he received the Royal Victorian Order of Great Britain, the Golden Palms and Rosetti of the French Academy, and the Cross of Merit of the Academy of Arts, Sciences, and Literature of Hainault, Belgium.

The generally dim view of America's literary past might be summed up in a sentence from Waldo Frank's *Our America* (1919): "Cultural America in 1900 was an untracked wilderness but dimly blazed by the heroic ax of Whitman." [10] H. L. Mencken preached similar views. In *A Book of Prefaces* (1917) he cited Whitman as the only nineteenth-century American writer offering "a courageous challenge to the intolerable prudishness and dirty-mindedness of Puritanism. . . ." [11] Mencken dismissed Hawthorne as a writer who "turned backward to the Puritans and Plymouth Rock." Today, even undergraduates quickly discover that Hawthorne was almost obsessively concerned with the very modern problem of dehumanized science. In the 1940s Dr. C. P. Obendorf demonstrated that in *The Scarlet Letter* Hawthorne had outlined the theory of psychosomatic medicine and had anticipated much of the psychoanalytic technique. [12]

As for Emerson whose doctrines helped to mold Thoreau, Whitman, Charles W. Eliot, John Dewey, and the American college, Mencken remarked that "Emerson took flight from earth altogether.* What one notices about him chiefly is his lack of influence upon the mainstream of American thought, such as it is." This was echoed by Waldo Frank: "The true motif of Emerson is an hysterical plea . . . the world he knew was so wholly measured by materialistic standards that it did not occur to him to find his heaven save in the air: place his 'over-soul' among the stars." [13] This of the man who said, "Give me insight into today and you may keep all past and future worlds," the man who argued that America could be transformed by fresh and bold thinking. Obviously such snap judgments about Emerson grew not out of careful reading but from the picking up of a phrase like "the over-soul." Nor did

---

* Mencken and Frank were apparently unaware of Emerson's *English Traits*, a penetrating analysis of Victorian England, and using materials from geography, history, literature, education, sociology, and economics. The book is filled with statistics.

these critics recognize in that concept the ancient and honorable Platonic tradition which had permeated English poetry from Spenser to Wordsworth.

Mencken's arch enemy, Paul Elmer More, wrote far more perceptively about Hawthorne than did the iconoclasts. More recognized the American tradition of darkness, stemming from the forest as well as the contemplation of guilt and sin, a "tradition" which embraced the Salem witch trials, the gothic novels of Charles Brockden Brown, the poetry of Freneau, and the tales of Poe. As Ludwig Lewisohn remarked: "More had not impartially read any book written later than 1890, Mencken had read hardly a book written before that date. Both men are at once monsters of ignorance and monsters of learning." [14]

The ignorance of America's literary past appears in Dreiser's essay, "Life, Art and America," published in *The Seven Arts,* whose editors were Randolph Bourne, Waldo Frank and Van Wyck Brooks. [15] Dreiser rightly pointed out that America had produced no philosopher of the first rank; no historian equal to a Grote or a Gibbon; no critic of the stature of Taine or Sainte-Beuve; no dramatist such as Ibsen, Chekhov or Shaw. But he got on more shaky ground in saying we had no novelist equal to de Maupassant; no poet, save Edgar Lee Masters, since Whitman. "In painting a Whistler, an Innes, a Sargent. Who else?"

Dreiser's omissions are significant: he did not mention Hawthorne, Melville, Thoreau, Emily Dickinson, or Henry James. In painting he seemed ignorant of Copley, Morse, Ryder, Eakins, and Homer. Like most of his contemporary critics he used Whistler's expatriation as an indictment of America—all of them forgetting or ignorant of the fact that Whistler was largely brought up in Europe. America was only technically his homeland.

There were a variety of causes for such widespread ignorance of the American cultural past, probably the most important being the academic establishment. Before the 1920s, college courses in American literature were rare, and were usually looked down upon by the professorial hierarchy. Even those professors who examined the subject were likely to bow to the courtly muses of Europe. Speaking of the Harvard he knew from 1904 to 1907, Brooks said it was "up in all things European" but had no place for Americanism; there Americanism meant Philistinism.

Harvard Professor Barrett Wendell's *A Literary History of America* (1900) devoted a single sentence to Melville, quoting Robert Louis Stevenson in praise of Melville's books on the South Seas. Thoreau was treated in a chapter entitled "The Lesser Men of Concord," in which Wendell made the incredible statement that Thoreau "was no immortal maker of phrases." [16] As for Hawthorne, " 'The Marble Faun' is our only indication of what he might have done if his sensitive youth had been exposed to the unfathomably human influence of Europe." There are scattered references to *Huckleberry Finn,* two of them commenting on the "grotesque" title. As for Whitman's *Crossing Brooklyn Ferry,* it was "confused, inarticulate, and surging in a mad kind of rhythm which sounds as if hexameters were trying to bubble through sewage." [17]

Wendell's colleague, Professor Charles Eliot Norton, was even more exclusive in his tastes in American literature: he thought that an American Men of Letters series would run to no more than three.[18] Similarly Henry Adams, according to Brooks, was unaware of Emily Dickinson and Stephen Crane, of Winslow Homer and Albert Ryder.[19] It is no wonder that Malcolm Cowley said that the colleges, with their emphasis upon the European past, failed to give a sense of American history and society.[20]

According to Howard Mumford Jones, the only professor of American Literature until 1917 seems to have been William B. Cairns at the University of Wisconsin, at which time Fred Lewis Pattee was given a similar title at Penn State.[21] Even as late as the mid-1930s a Princeton doctoral examination in English contained no question on American literature.

Thus any knowledge of the American cultural past had to be largely a do-it-yourself achievement. Brooks remarked that the literary rebels of the 1920s had "seldom read any American books but *Moby Dick* and *Huckleberry Finn.*"[22] Floyd Dell described the typical attitude of the literary authorities toward American literature: Whitman was "the good gray poet;" Emerson the author of a poem about a mountain and a squirrel; Thoreau a "Nature-Lover." "The educational authorities did not want us to know the truth about American Literature. They were afraid that the real Emerson and Thoreau and Phillips and Whittier and Whitman would corrupt our young minds. So we were left to discover them for ourselves—*which all too frequently we failed to do.*" [Ital. mine.][23]

A notable exception to this kind of ignorance was John Macy's *The Spirit of American Literature,* first published in 1908 and revised in 1912. Macy found Hawthorne to be "less provincial in a derogatory sense than his charming biographer, Mr. James" when one compared Hawthorne's American notes on England with James' British notes on America [*The American Scene*]. More important Macy praised such novels as *Moby Dick, The Story of a Country Town,* and those of Harold Frederic and Stephen Crane.

As so often happens when intellectuals have shallow roots in the past, the critics of the new renaissance tended to be doctrinaire. They made generalizations based upon theory rather than upon careful examination of evidence. Depending upon their various predilections they interpreted American literature and society in terms of Nietzschean, Marxist, or Freudian categories. It was not until Vernon Louis Parrington's *Main Currents in American Thought* (1927–1930) that a major critic fully recognized the native Jeffersonian tradition. Before Parrington, Whitman was usually treated as a kind of literary sport. A full length critical and biographical study of Melville did not appear until Lewis Mumford's *Herman Melville* in 1929.* As far as literary studies were concerned, Jefferson and Lincoln might never have existed as part of the pattern of our cultural heritage. As will appear, Beard dealt with the founding fathers in Marxist terms; Mencken saw the American people through the eyes of Nietzsche; and nearly everyone had a field day with Freud in dealing with Puritanism and in debunking our political and literary heroes.

One of the monuments in this cemetery of the American past was Van Wyck Brooks; *The Ordeal of Mark Twain* (1920). Starting with the premise that "a sort of unconscious conspiracy actuated all America against the creative spirit," [24] he arrived at the conclusion that Mark Twain "is the supreme victim of an epoch in American history. . . ." [25] The villains of the tragedy were American business, Mrs. Clemens, and William Dean Howells. Whenever objective evidence was lacking Brooks resorted to amateur Freudian speculation on Twain's motivations.

---

* The first biography of Melville was Raymond Weaver's *Melville; Mariner and Mystic* (1921).

Brooks accepted and perpetuated contemporary clichés about nineteenth-century America. In an age glorified by "the beautiful anger of the Tolstoys, the Marxes, the Nietzsches, the Renans, the Ruskins and the Morrises— in that age America, innocent and profoundly untroubled, slept the righteous sleep of its own manifest and peculiar destiny." [26] Thus by pluralizing one Russian, two Germans, one Frenchman and two Englishmen, and by omitting not only Thoreau, Whittier, Whitman's *Democratic Vistas*, Edward Bellamy, and Henry George, but also such voices of protest as Harriet Beecher Stowe, William Lloyd Garrison, Margaret Fuller, Hamlin Garland, and William Dean Howells' *A Traveller from Altruria* he loaded the dice. As for Twain's own anger with "the damned human race," that was merely the result of the suppression of the artist in the man. In Brooks' view "Twain cannot be called a satirist." [27]

For Brooks the really tragic fate was to be a humorist: ". . . the role of humorist was foreign to [Twain's] nature. . . . For obviously the making of the humorist was the undoing of the artist. It meant the suppression of his aesthetic desires, the degradation of everything in his own nature, upon which the creative instinct feeds. . . ." However, the factual evidence presented in the book suggests that aesthetic desires rarely prompted Twain to write; the need for money did. Thus it was only when his publishers suggested that he write about his adventures in the West that he set to work on *Roughing It*. Twain's repeated statement shows that his aesthetic desires had been most satisfied by his life as a pilot. For Brooks even "His choice of a pen name . . . proved how urgently he felt the need of a protective coloration in this society where the writer was a despised type." [28] This of the man whose pseudonym was about as much protective coloration as was Buffalo Bill's. Certainly in nineteenth-century America Irving,* Cooper, Emerson, Bryant, Poe, Longfellow, Whittier, Lowell, and Holmes could scarcely be described as despised types. From Andrew Jackson to Theodore Roosevelt, Presidents had welcomed writers to the White House; they offered diplomatic posts to Irving, Hawthorne, Bancroft, Motley, Bayard Taylor, Lowell, Howells, and Mark Twain—in a number of cases the most important ministries in Europe. Twain became so prominent that he traveled under incognitos and signed hotel registers with names like J. P. Smith and J. P. Jones. A steamboat was named for him; he was honored at banquets and public ceremonies; his work was published in *The Atlantic* and *Century;* Yale and The University of Missouri gave him honorary degrees. He was Grant's friend and publisher; Andrew Carnegie sent him barrels of whiskey, and Henry H. Rogers, a mogul of Standard Oil, helped him out of bankruptcy. In London he was sought out by Browning, Turgenev, Herbert Spencer, Trollope, Wilkie Collins, and Lewis Carroll. Oxford gave him an honorary degree in 1907.

Like Brooks' theme of the despised writer his diatribes against Howells and Olivia Clemens have a doctrinaire quality. Both people are excoriated for urging Twain to tone down certain passages. Typical is the comment, without evidence, that Mrs. Clemens no doubt thought of Huck Finn as "that disreputable, illiterate little boy." [29] (In point of fact she referred to him as "dear old Huck.")

---

* When Irving returned after seventeen years in Europe a great reception and public dinner was given for him in the New York City Hall. Those who could not get in could read the speeches in the newspapers. Plaster busts of Irving were sold by the hundreds at $15 each. James O. Hart, *The Popular Book,* N. Y., 1950, p. 84.

Brooks spoke of Twain's "lifetime of moral slavery." But when Mark let himself go as in *1601,* Brooks found it "a fetid stream of meaningless ribaldry—the waste of priceless psychic material." Here again is the myopia of the period which found prudery only in America. There is never any recognition of the fact that certain reticences were required of any nineteenth-century writer who hoped for publication in English. As Justin Kaplan has shown, Twain's humor was sometimes of the back-house variety. Such emendations as Howells advised tended to be in the nature of minor cuts, like the shortening of a scene where Becky gazes at a "stark naked" figure in an anatomy textbook or the omission of a phrase about a dog who having sat on a beetle, let out a yelp and "went sailing up the aisle, his tail shut down like a hasp." Awfully good but a little too dirty," * said Howells. This kind of squeamishness had its British counterpart: the editor of an English magazine asked Hardy to change a scene where Angel Clare carries the dairymaids across a flooded lane; the editor suggested that it would be better if the girls could be transported in a wheelbarrow.

It is true that Howells was abnormally prudish, but to his credit he published Twain and Bret Harte in *The Atlantic.* If anything he tended to overpraise Twain, calling him "perhaps the greatest humorist who ever lived." Certainly Twain was not working under much prudish restraint when with Charles Dudley Warner he wrote *The Gilded Age.* It is significant that in discussing the book Brooks implied that Twain was responsible for some of the genteel sections that are the work of Warner.

* Kaplan quotes Holmes in *Elsie Venner:* a dog who goes "bundling out of the open school-house door with a most pitiable yelp, and his stump of a tail shut down as close as his owner ever shut the short, stubbed blade of his jack-knife." Kaplan, 193n.

Yet so enduring has been the Brooks myth that as late as 1966 Justin Kaplan in his biography of Twain felt it necessary to refute "the familiar claim that Livy and her circle exerted an influence on Mark Twain that was genteel to the point of emasculation." [30] The facts are that Mrs. Clemens and Mrs. Warner suggested that their husbands stop aimless talking and embody their ideas in a novel. The ladies were consulted all through its composition and made the final decision about which several possible conclusions should be used. As Kaplan says, *"The Gilded Age . . .* is not hushed and polite literature, nor does it deal with the smiling aspects of American life."

In fact it would be hard to imagine a more cynical picture of American business, politics, and sex. Almost everyone is represented as having some scheme to make a quick fortune either through speculation in railroad lands or through porkbarrel legislation. In the House and Senate the price for the majority vote of a committee is $10,000 plus another $10,000 for each chairman. A Senator or Representative with moral pretensions cost $3,000, a small-fry country member about $500.

Nor do Twain and Warner pull their punches about sexual shenanigans. Laura, who had been tricked into a bogus marriage with Colonel Selby, and had been deserted, finds on his reappearance that she still passionately wants him:

> Was not her love for George Selby deeper than any other woman's could be? Had she not a right to him? Did he not belong to her by virtue of her overmastering passion? His wife—she was not his wife, except by law. She could not be. Even with the law she could have no right to stand between two souls that were one. . . .

She may have heard, doubtless she had, similar theories that were prevalent at that day, theories of the tyranny of marriage and of the freedom of marriage. She had even heard women lecturers say that marriage should only continue so long as it pleased either party to it—for a year, a month, or a day. . . .

Indeed in that very house had she not heard women prominent before the country and besieging Congress, utter sentiments that fully justified the course she was making out for herself.*

Eventually Laura murders Colonel Selby and is triumphantly acquitted, chiefly because of her beauty. When she is freed, seven men, some of them prominent, propose marriage.

Granted that Twain and Warner were satirizing certain facets of American life, the point is that the novel does not support Brooks' thesis that the prudishness of Mrs. Clemens prevented her husband from dealing frankly with life. In fact, Kaplan presents evidence to show that her standards of literary decorum differed little from her husband's.

Whatever toning down Howells and Olivia Clemens may have advised in *Huckleberry Finn*, it was still too realistic for many readers. The Springfield *Republican* attacked both *Tom Sawyer* and *Huckleberry Finn* as immoral; the Boston *Transcript* said that the latter was "so flat as well as coarse, that nobody wants to read it;"

---

* In 1871 Victoria Woodhull, speaking in Steinway Hall said: "Yes I am a free lover! I have an inalienable, constitutional, and natural right to love whom I may, to love as long or as short a period as I can, to change that love every day if I please!"

Earlier that year she had appeared before the Judiciary Committee of the House of Representatives to argue for women's suffrage. Johanna Johnston, *Mrs. Satan*, New York, 1967, pp. 133 and 87.

the Committee of the Public Library of Concord banned it from their shelves. For another forty years it was usually excluded from Sunday School libraries and frowned upon by schoolmarms. It is ironic that in recent years the book which bitterly satirizes the attitude of white Southerners toward the Negro should be under attack because of its realistic use of the word *nigger* in contexts where it would certainly have been used.

There were of course tragic elements in Twain's life; his mercurial temperament which led him into all sorts of abortive schemes; his masochistic streak; and a long series of family illness and early deaths. He outlived his beloved wife and all but one of his children. Far from being the dedicated literary artist betrayed by society and associates, Twain tended to interrupt his writing to embark upon any scheme that came into his head.

The importance of *The Ordeal of Mark Twain* is that it is so typical of the literary criticism of its era. Instead of being a scholarly attempt to discover and evaluate the evidence, it is propaganda: the marshalling of selected evidence to support a doctrinaire thesis. It was part of the contemporary war on Puritanism, business, and the alleged American hostility to the artist. On its publication Mark Van Doren in *The Nation* hailed it as a "brilliant book [which] comes so near the truth." [31] He deplored only an overseriousness. As Alfred Kazin said of Brooks: "In his *The Ordeal of Mark Twain,* particularly, he gave the twenties the image of the Gilded Age that lies at the heart of that whole sentimental pathetic conception of the artist in America which dominated the critical opinion of the time." [32]

The irony is that from the early writings of Brooks to the Nobel prize speech of Sinclair Lewis in 1930, the rebels against the genteel tradition accepted a view of our literary situation promulgated by their bête noire, William Dean Howells. In an unfortunate chapter in *Criticism and Fiction* (1892) Howells had defended the prudishness of the British and American novel on the grounds that it was addressed to a mixed company, the vast majority of whom were ladies, and that "many, if not most, of these ladies are young girls." He argued that "any author who will deal with guilty love intrigue holds all readers in his hand, the highest with the lowest, as long as he hints at the slightest hope of the smallest potential naughtiness." And he, of course, was responsible for the theory that novelists should deal with "the more smiling aspects of American life." Obviously such views lent support to Brooks' theory that Howells must have had a baleful effect on his friend Twain.

The theory seemed to justify the contention of the iconoclasts that American life and literature were in the grip of Puritanism.

2.

The Crepe-Hung Plug Hat

The seventeenth-century Puritans had been haunted by visions of the Devil; the writers of the first third of the twentieth century were haunted by the specter of the Puritan. But it was not so much the Puritan of historic record that bedeviled the imagination of these writers as it was a kind of intellectual construct. At times this symbol became almost as much a caricature as Rollin Kirby's famous cartoon figure wearing the undertaker's coat, crepe-hung stovepipe hat, and carrying a badly furled umbrella. Especially after the coming of Prohibition, the symbol became as real to the age as was a witch to Cotton Mather. Some of the writing on the Puritan might have used Mather's title, *Wonders of the Invisible World.*

Three of the writers who helped to create the twentieth-century image of the Puritan were Van Wyck Brooks, Randolph Bourne and H. L. Mencken. Within a decade they had been joined by a pack in full cry. However, this twentieth-century construct has little in common with William Bradford, Nathaniel Ward, or Cotton Mather, and bears no resemblance to Anne Hutchinson or Roger Williams.

The harsh aspects of the historic Puritan had long before been portrayed by Hawthorne. As early as 1835 he had written:

> Not far from Merry Mount was a settlement of Puritans, most dismal wretches, who said their prayers before daylight, and wrought in the forest or cornfield till evening made it prayer time again. Their weapons were always at hand to shoot down the straggling savage. When they met in conclave, it was never to keep up the old English mirth, but to hear sermons three hours long, or to proclaim bounties on the heads of wolves and the scalps of Indians. Their festivals were fast days, and their chief pastime the singing of psalms. Woe to the youth or maiden who did but dream of a dance! The selectman nodded to the constable: and there sat the light-heeled reprobate in the stocks: or if he danced, it was round the whipping-post, which might be termed the Puritan Maypole.

From this historic Puritan later writers extrapolated certain aspects which they said represented the Puritan elements in modern life. Or perhaps more often they pinned the label on those aspects of modern America which they disliked. At the very start of *The Wine of the Puritans* Brooks attacked neither their bigotry nor harsh-noted he then represented Whittier and Holmes as preaching these virtues exclusively. With his "heads I win, tails you lose" logic he contended that "Americans are excessively rational," and then attacked Transcendentalism as an escape from the rational.

> Emerson and his followers represent the despair of explaining the world in general (which had opened to them) by the rational philosophy they were accustomed to apply to the provincial life of New England in particular. And so they threw aside the hope of any rational explanation at all and sought to interpret life in arbitrary and purely spiritual terms. Emerson is a lofty and inspired sophist . . . whose sophism is the direct result of a provincial training, rational as an explanation of the peculiar life in one corner of the world. . . .[1]

Now whatever one may think of the attempt to explain the world in purely spiritual terms, one has to be oblivious to the whole history of religious mysticism to pinpoint this as a provincial New England abberation. Even the most superficial student of Emerson can trace his transcendentalism directly to Wordsworth, and beyond that to Plato and the Vedas. It was not his "provincial training" that led him to his interpretation of the world; it was his admiration for Wordsworth, Coleridge, and Carlyle—all of whom he hunted up in England.

As the passage on Emerson demonstrates, Brooks was never very clear about what he meant by Puritanism; he used it as an epithet in much the way a right-winger now uses *Communism*. However, it seemed to mean to him the sum of those forces hostile to the artist. Americans "cannot accept the arts of life. You can be enthusiastic and extravagant about them but you cannot accept them as perfectly normal, natural elements of civilized life." [2] Ten years later he was harping on the same theme:

And observe the condition in which we now are: sultry, flaccid, not knowing what we want and incapable of wanting anything very much, certainly not in love with life. . . . A universal tepidity . . . the faded offspring of the Puritan hatred of human nature, which makes a majority of our kindly fellow countrymen incapable of living, loving, thinking, dreaming or hoping with any degree of passion or intensity. . . .[3]

Obviously this tepid America—if indeed it existed during the years of World War I—is far different from the intensity of the historic Puritan. And for all of Brooks' brave words about human nature, love and passion, he was himself rather squeamish about these matters. His distaste for Twain's *1601* has already been mentioned; when *Winesburg, Ohio* appeared, he called Anderson "a phallic Chekhov." In a letter dated August 1920 Anderson told Brooks:

It did hurt, though, when I found you also rather taking Winesburg, for example, as a sex book. It got under my hide a bit. . . .[4]

Brooks' colleague on *The Seven Arts,* Randolph Bourne, better understood both the dynamism of Puritanism and its sexual aspects. In an essay "The Puritan's Will to Power" he gave a Freudian explanation:

Instincts and impulses, in the puritan, are not miraculously cancelled, but have their full play. The primitive currents of life are not blocked and turned back on their sources, but turned into powerful and usually devastating channels.[5]

Like Brooks he saw the Puritan as hostile to art and the full life. "He [the Puritan] first scares [people] into abandoning the rich and sensuous and expressive impulses in life, and then teaches them to be proud of having done so." [6] Therefore ". . . the puritan always needs to be thoroughly explained and exposed. We must keep him before our eyes, recognize him as the real enemy. . . ."

Waldo Frank, another of the *Seven Arts* group, saw this enemy lurking behind every machine. "Industrialism is the new Puritanism. . . ." The whole of *Our America* (1919) written, he said, to explain America to the French is the kind of diatribe which helped to create in the minds of Europeans a stereotype they have never entirely got over. Like Brooks, Frank spoke of "the bitter wreckage of [Twain's] long life." As has been noted he pictured Emerson as a hysterical escapee from American life. "New England is a tragedy of ambition. . . . Insanity is common. Neurosis is birthright." [7] Frost's poetry represented "at most a sardonic humor of resignation." [8] Henry Adams was "archetypal. And a whole starved and miserable race of brilliant men moves with his words." [9]

H. L. Mencken, who took an equally dim view of American culture, found it amusing rather than tragic. In answer to a question about why he stayed in the United States, he replied, "Why do men go to zoos?" For him also Puritanism was a chief villain. In "Puritanism as a Literary Force," he wrote:

> Naturally enough, this moral obsession has given a strong colour to American literature. In truth, it has coloured it so brilliantly, that American literature is set off sharply from all other literatures. In none other will you find so wholesale and ecstatic a sacrifice

of aesthetic ideas, of all the fine gusto of passion and beauty, to notions of what is meet, proper and nice.[10]

Even the conservative *North American Review* joined in the chorus. In March 1915 Louise Collier Willcox, writing on Thomas Hardy, said that one of the reasons America had not and apparently could not produce a great literature such as Russia, France, England, Germany, and Italy had done was that "we are suffering from nervous exhaustion and strain brought about by Puritan intensity and strain, and have not the vitality or vigor to face reality." [11] Here, of course, is the familiar only-in-America cliché and a glance into the distorting rear-view mirror. When one ponders the generalizations, the question occurs about the greatness of Italian literature during the preceding century, or for that matter how many German literary figures since Goethe were more important than Emerson, Hawthorne, Thoreau, Melville, Whitman, Twain, and James?

One of the most intemperate attacks upon Puritanism as the source of all evils was *In the American Grain* (1925) by William Carlos Williams. Unwittingly falling in with the New England historians of our literature he saw in the Mayflower "the character of the beginnings in North America." But for Williams ". . . it is sordid that a rich world should follow apathetically after. Their misfortune has became a malfesant [sic] ghost that dominates us all. . . . And it is still to-day the Puritan who keeps his frightened grip upon the throat of the world lest it should prove him—empty."

The result of this Puritan spirit was that it "has produced a race incapable of flower." In a vast oversimplification of social forces he blamed all our national ills on Puritanism:

[America] has become the most lawless country in the world, a panorama of murders, perversions, a terrific ungoverned strength, excusable only because of the horrid beauty of its great machines. To-day it is a generation of gross know-nothingism, of blackened churches where hymns groan like chants from stupified jungles. . . .[12]

This race incapable of flower had in the preceding ten years produced a revolution in poetry; the year in which Williams made his statement was a vintage one for the American novel. The Europe in which he was temporarily living was in economic chaos following the senseless slaughter of fifteen million people; Mussolini and Stalin were in power and Hitler was on the march.

In addition to disregarding the darker side of European civilization, these only-in-America critics forgot both the experience of European writers and the existence of a considerable body of un-Puritanical American literature. They overlooked the fact that in France Flaubert had been prosecuted and nearly convicted for the alleged immorality of *Madame Bovary* and that Baudelaire had been convicted on a similar charge; that Ibsen's *Ghosts* and *The Doll's House* had raised a storm in Norway and England; and that Hardy's *Jude the Obscure* was according to Florence Hardy, subjected to an "onslaught . . . started by the vituperative section of the press—unequaled in violence since the publication of Swinburne's *Poems and Ballads* thirty years before—[and] taken up by anonymous writers of libelous letters and postcards. . . ." * [13] When D. H. Lawrence's *The Rainbow* was published, the self-styled Public Morality Council of London instituted a police

---

* Florence Hardy's biography was largely the autobiography of Thomas Hardy written for posthumous publication.

prosecution. English law permitted any magistrate to order the suppression of a book on his own authority.[14]

It could even be argued that nineteenth-century American writers ventured into areas normally closed to their British contemporaries. Whitman is a case in point. Henry Adams showed a superficial knowledge of American literature when he stated that the only American writers he could think of who had insisted on the power of sex as every classic had done were Walt Whitman and Bret Harte "as far as the magazines would let him venture." He obviously forgot Hawthorne. In an era when Emma Bovary and Anna Karenina had to die in atonement for their sins, Hawthorne's Hester emerged as morally superior to those around her. To Arthur Dimnesdale she says, "We are not the worst of sinners. What we did had a kind of consecration of its own." And in *The Blithedale Romance* (1883) Zenobia is so sexy that Miles Coverdale felt compelled sometimes to close his eyes "as if it were not quite the privilege of modesty to gaze at her." He could not help thinking that she was a woman who "had lived and loved," to whom wedlock "had thrown wide the gates of mystery."

On a far lower literary level there was George Lippard's *The Quaker City*—a novel which perhaps gave Philadelphia its enduring nickname. The opening chapters describe a luxurious bordello and gambling house frequented by judges, lawyers, doctors, merchants, an editor and a parson. Lippard, a reporter, got the idea for the novel from a trial he had covered. A young man had shot a wealthy playboy who had taken the defendant's sister to a brothel where he seduced her. Lippard's outrage at the way upper-class men preyed on working girls did not prevent him from making the seduction scenes highly voluptuous. First published in ten installments in 1844, it appeared in book form a year later. Within four years it went through thirty editions. Its sale of 60,000 copies was the largest in America before the appearance of *Uncle Tom's Cabin.*[15]

Then there was John William DeForest's excellent *Miss Ravenel's Conversion* (1887), a novel praised by Howells. In it Dr. Ravenel, sent to New Orleans, is welcomed by a half-drunken Union officer, who occupies a beautiful house built and furnished for a Parisian actress by a man who is now a Confederate captain. Dr. Ravenel's friend, Colonel Carter of the Union Army, maintains "the prettiest little French *boudoir.*" The *"boudoir* business was so awfully common in the world as then constituted, that men who engaged in it could not well be ostracised from society."

Later, on a boat Colonel Carter meets a charming widow, Mrs. Larue,* a woman who thinks that "Don Juan was a model man." The colonel had been drinking but "She was tolerably well accustomed to drunken gentlemen, and was not easily hurt by love-making, no matter how vigorous." A chaplain, impressed by her discussions of religion, "may also have been pleased with her plump shoulders and round arms, and he certainly did glance at them occasionally as their outlines showed through the transparent muslin. . . ."

It is significant that neither Mrs. Larue nor Colonel Carter is represented as a moral leper. The Colonel refuses to descend to the well-known trickery of getting public property condemned to auction and then buying it for a song, and he is deeply shocked when the Governor, for political reasons, promotes the coward, Gazaway; whereas

* Howells later remembered her as "a very lurid Mrs. Leroy, of whom I cannot think without shuddering." *Heroines of Fiction*, II, 157, N. Y., 1901.

the Governor would have been shocked by Carter's affair with Mrs. Larue.

DeForest was satiric about New England Puritans. As for those of the past Dr. Ravenel muses, "Dead as they are, they govern the continent. At the same time they must have been disagreeable to live with." Not that DeForest glamorized the South with "the whiskey drinking, negro-whipping, man-slaughtering ruffians in Louisiana with their revolvers, bowie knives, black wives and mulatto children." When Dr. Ravenel is clouted on the head in the streets, he remarks, "I knew I was in New Orleans when I was hit, just as a shipwrecked man knew he was in a Christian country when he saw a gallows." Certainly *Miss Ravenel's Conversion* does not fit Mencken's description of American literature as sacrificing everything "to notions of what is meet, proper and nice." As Gordon Haight points out in his introduction to the Rinehart edition of 1955, the book is at times more realistic than *The Red Badge of Courage*.

However DeForest was not the only novelist of his time whose work refutes Henry Adams on the puritan sexlessness of American literature. In 1887—the date of *Miss Ravenel*—Harold Frederic published *Seth's Brother's Wife* in which Isobel, a bored wife, carries on a dangerous flirtation with her naive young brother-in-law, Seth. The husband, Albert, coming home unexpectedly, interrupts a seduction scene. When Albert is murdered for a sum of money he is carrying to pay a bribe for his nomination to Congress, Isobel assumes that Seth did it for her sake. In order to hold onto him she even tries to break up his engagement to a childhood sweetheart. In a still better novel, *The Damnation of Theron Ware* (1896) Frederic portrayed a young Methodist clergyman temporarily deserting his wife to chase off after the tremendously and wilfully seductive Celia Madden. The novel also gives a thoroughly cynical picture of puritanical Protestantism. It is a far better novel than *Elmer Gantry* of a generation later. Although Anthony Comstock succeeded in keeping *Theron Ware* out of the mails, it made the best-seller list in the year of its publication.[16]

A considerably less skillful novel, Hamlin Garland's *Rose of Dutcher's Cooly* (1895), tells how a farmer's daughter learns about barnyard sex. Garland remarks that "these happenings have a terrible power to stir and develop passions prematurely." In the story, children write obscene words on fences and little girls scream such words at each other. Early marriages are the result of "the mere brute passion which seizes so many boys and girls at that age [in their teens]." After some sort of rural sexual experience Rose goes to the University of Wisconsin where she discovers that she has a mind. Later she meets the sophisticated Dr. Isobel Herrick who "knew men as polygamous by instinct, insatiable as animals. . . ." Through Isobel, Rose meets interesting people and ends by marrying a man who appreciates an intelligent woman. The novel is essentially about the contrast between the crude sexuality of the country and the civilized attitudes of the city.

And of course there was Stephen Crane's *Maggie, A Girl of the Streets,* privately printed in 1893 and published commercially three years later. It is a thoroughly naturalistic study of the forces which create a prostitute. Edward Wagenknecht argues that it was not the Puritanism of editors and critics which prevented recognition of *Maggie* but the immaturity of the work itself.[17] Nevertheless Robert Spiller states that with its republication in 1896 "modern American fiction was born." [18]

It is of course quite true that during those years there was a great deal of genteel literature by such writers as F. Marion Crawford, F. Hopkinson Smith, Paul Leicester Ford, and Winston Churchill, and on a higher level by William Dean Howells and Henry James. But even James could represent Lambert Strether (almost his alter ego) as pleading with Chad Newsome not to desert his mistress, Mme. de Vionnet.

Yet even John Macy, who praised Thoreau, Whitman, and Twain as "our most stalwart men of genius," could say, "American literature is on the whole idealistic, sweet, delicate, nicely finished. There is little of it which might not have appeared in the *Youth's Companion*." [19] He failed to mention that there was little nineteenth-century British literature which would have been banned from a Sunday-School library—the usual fate of *The Scarlet Letter* and *Huckleberry Finn*. However in a passage obviously written in 1912 Macy, after praising Frank Norris, *Moby Dick, The Story of a Country Town,* Harold Frederic and Stephen Crane, commented, "However, a contemporary literature that includes Mrs. Wharton's 'Ethan Frome' and Mr. Dreiser's 'Jeannie Gerhardt,' both published last year, is not to be despaired of." Macy was of course right about the namby-pamby quality of later nineteenth-century American poetry and the triviality of the drama, but his own list of novelists is partial refutation of his charge that American literature was on the whole sweet and delicate. To his credit Macy did not lash the Puritan scapegoat—after all *sweet* and *delicate* are adjectives that hardly apply to the historic Puritan although Mencken had charged Puritanism with foisting upon American literature "notions of what is meet, proper and nice."

Of course there were squeamish and puritanical people who were shocked by *The Scarlet Letter, Huckleberry*

Finn, Miss Ravenel's Conversion and *The Damnation of Theron Ware* but the sales figures of these books indicate that there were also a great many people ready to buy and read them.

Mencken was on firmer ground when he brought charges against the literary establishment of critics, editors, and professors. Barrett Wendell's low view of Whitman is a case in point. The squeamish emendations to Twain's work by Gilder and Howells have already been cited. In fact Howells became the favorite target of the anti-Puritans.

In many ways Howells was an easy target. Despite his championship of DeForest, Fuller, Garland, Frederic, Crane and Norris and his early recognition of Twain as a major writer, he made some of the most prudish critical statements on record, and his own novels show an almost pathological squeamishness about sex.*

However some of Howells' mawkishness had been recognized long before Mencken, Brooks, and their followers took up the cry. A writer in *Lippincott's Monthly Magazine* of 1886 said that the one type of woman Howells seemed to approve was one "with seven different varieties of fool in her. . . ." For instance, "The wives lightly sketched in 'Private Theatricals' and 'Dr. Breen's Practice' are, indeed, rich chiefly in headaches, and nervous troubles, and their world does not seem much wider than that of an Oriental." [20]

By the time the iconoclasts raised their hue and cry against him, Howells was an old man, and despite his

---

* For instance in *Indian Summer* Imogene meets her fiancé Colville in the hall and "sweetly kissed him." "Coleville went out into the sunlight feeling like some strange, newly invented kind of scoundrel. . . ." "He was the bethrothed lover of this poor child [she is 20], whose affection he could not check without a degree of brutality for which only a better man would have had the courage."

occupancy of *Harper's* "Easy Chair," he was clearly a voice from the past. Even magazine stories were no longer reticent enough to suit him. In his column for March 1913 (he was then seventy-six) he complained:

> As yet their authors have not conceived of decently leaving the reader to suppose the clasping and kissing which perhaps goes on in life, and which their illustrators graphically report in embraces as frank as those of the lovers on the benches in the Park.[21]

In August of the same year he wrote nostalgically of Longfellow, Lowell, Whittier, Emerson and Hawthorne. "The clear, cold voice of Emerson called from the crystal air of Concord in duteous accents which we seem to fail of in the voices of Indianapolis and our other literary centers." [22] Literature was already ceasing to be puritanical enough for his taste.

In all periods of rapid social change there are those who speak with alarm. The very intensity of the cries of the conservatives is in itself testimony to the success of the revolt against the genteel tradition. As one would expect, the voices were mixed: it cannot be said that a single point of view was dominant. Thus in 1915 the politically conservative *North American Review* carried an article in praise of Whitman; whereas the supposedly liberal *New Republic* published an editorial praising Anthony Comstock, and saying "No one who doesn't know how such things [possibly things like *Fanny Hill*] were thrust on young people some forty or fifty years ago, and how difficult and risky the trade has been made nowadays, can realize the vast amount of good Mr. Comstock has accomplished." [23] However three months later a tongue-in-cheek editorial praised Comstock for bringing Margaret Sanger's pamphlet on birth control to public notice.[24]

The debate over birth control was of course related to the controversy about sex in literature. The *New Republic,* which was friendly to the views of Margaret Sanger, nevertheless published in 1915 an article-length "Communication" by a Florence Wyman entitled "The Revolt of Wives." [25] In it she attacked "the sensualities of marriage." The root evil was the "abnormal, inordinate, insane sensuality primarily of men." She asserted that "Women are beginning to feel that if marriage is not relieved of an impurity which is essentially that of prostitution, it is not good enough for them nor the daughters they love. . . ." *

In subsequent numbers at least two ladies took issue with this view, whereas a gentleman said that no one could read "The Revolt of Wives" without sympathy and admiration. "Sincerity and high courage vibrate in every sentence." [26]

That same year Randolph Bourne wrote for *The New Republic* a favorable review of Dreiser's *The Genius.* After commenting on the courage of the critic who "takes his life in his hands" to praise such a book, he stated "That Mr. Dreiser is our only novelist who tries to plumb below this conventional superstructure is his great distinction. . . ." [27]

But nine years later in that same periodical Mary Austin argued that because sex experience for women always had shadows of pain, death, and the symbol of life, "the bawdy joke must always remain taboo in the presence of the better sort of women" [28]—a statement which in 1924 obviously excluded a large portion of college girls from the better sort of women.

---

* By contrast in the 1870s Victoria Woodhull, addressing a Spiritualist convention in Chicago, said, "Every man should have thundered in his ears the need for the female orgasm." Johnston, p. 206.

As late as 1925 *The Atlantic* published Ellen Duvall's attack on modern literature entitled "The New Paganism," somewhat mistakenly described by the editors as "sensible, fresh, and pithy." In it she said:

> Misled in part perhaps by Freudian psychology so-called,—which is no psychology at all, but simply a dull, materialistic theory of life based on animal instinct only,—our pagan fiction seems chiefly interested in man because of his capacity for concupiscence. . . .[29]

Such literature, she said, belonged on the other side of the channel with *Madame Bovary* and *L'Ile des pengouins*.

These defenders of Victorian standards were joined by an impressive group of college professors, such people as Paul Elmer More of Princeton, Irving Babbitt of Harvard, Brander Matthews of Columbia, William Lyon Phelps of Yale, Arthur Hobson Quinn of Pennsylvania, and Stuart Sherman of Iowa. For instance, More wrote, "For my part I still prefer James Russell Lowell's *Under the Willows* to the self-advertised passion of a certain living poetess who bears the same family name;" [30] Phelps told women's clubs that A. S. M. Hutchinson's *If Winter Comes* was a great modern novel, and stated that the award of the Nobel Prize to Sinclair Lewis was an insult to the United States; [31] Quinn in his *American Fiction* (1936) devoted a chapter to F. Marion Crawford but condensed David Graham Phillips, Dreiser, Lewis, Upton Sinclair and Sherwood Anderson into a single chapter; Babbitt hated everything after Rousseau. With some justice Mencken spoke of "the loud patriotic alarm of Dr. Stuart Sherman of Iowa, with his maxim that Puritanism is the official philosophy of America . . . and that all who dispute it are enemy aliens and should be deported." [32]

Like Howells, Sherman applauded certain qualities of the realists; he granted that the post-war soul-searching mood was tremendously good for the country. But his real feelings came out in his remarks on Dreiser, Hecht, Mencken and Lewis:

The monoptic or naturalistic vision and criticism of life are enjoying wide popularity because they are tremendously flattering to the lazy men and women who are out of their part; they confer a sense of superiority upon that indolent and inferior portion of mankind which slips and slumps from the great stage which tests a man's art, back into the subconventional, formless, unchanneled turmoil of instinct and passion.[33]

Sherman said of himself that he should not be considered as one of the "Propagandists, Prohibitionists, Prudes, Purists, Puritans and Professors" so much despised by what he called the literary "Mohawks," but his views certainly put him in some of those categories and his involved sentence structure revealed the professor. His nostalgia for the Genteel Tradition is apparent in his comment that Stevenson "was one of the most accomplished and versatile artists of the latter nineteenth century." But some modern things could be admired: Gluyas Williams' illustrations to Robert Benchley's writing were in Sherman's opinion "altogether unequalled since Raphael produced his Sistine Madonna." [34]

The case against the upholders of the Genteel Tradition—which the radicals equated with puritanism—would have been stronger except for three things: the Genteel-Puritan influence was far weaker than the iconoclasts charged; second their own literary judgments were often as fallible as were those of the enemy; and third they misunderstood the nature of the thing called Puritanism.

In their literary criticism the iconoclasts tended to evaluate writers on the basis of their anti-Puritan content. Not only did Mencken underestimate Emerson and Hawthorne, he lumped Howells with Henry James: ". . . both quickly showed that timorousness and reticence which are the distinguishing marks of the Puritan. . . . The American scene that they depicted with such meticulous care was chiefly peopled with marionettes." One might paraphrase W. C. Fields: Never give a Puritan an even break.

Mencken also equated Ellen Glasgow with Frances Hodgson Burnett, F. Hopkinson Smith and Alice Brown; Robert Frost was simply "Whittier without the whiskers." [35] Mencken then went on to praise Lizette Woodworth Reese, "who has written more sound poetry, more genuinely eloquent and beautiful poetry, than all the new poets put together—more than a whole posse of Masters and Lindsays, more than a hundred Amy Lowells. There are others, Neihardt and John McClure among them. . . ." [36] Granted that Lizette Woodworth Reese was a better poet than most of the lady versifiers with three-cylinder names who infested *The Atlantic, Harper's, Scribner's* and *The Century,* Mencken's enthusiasm was excessive. He excoriated Pattee's *A History of American Literature Since 1870* because among other things Pattee did not mention Harry Leon Wilson or George Ade. [37] As for James Branch Cabell, "His name is known today by every civilized American, and he is probably read and admired as widely as any other American author of his dignity." [38]

Cabell, like Dreiser, became a hero to the crusaders against Puritanism. The attacks upon *Jurgen* elevated that sophomoric snickering into a classic. Henry Seidel Canby stated that "Mr. Cabell has a fully matured style with body and beauty. . . ." [39] In a book on Cabell in 1925 Carl Van Doren announced, "Nor is it easy to resist the temptation to say, at the outset, that Mr. Cabell is already a classic if any American novelist of this century is." [40] Nor did Van Doren resist the temptation: *Jurgen* "is a continual delight," [41] and "There seems to be no longer any reason for not associating [Cabell] with the only comparable American romancers, Hawthorne and Melville." [42] Of the three Cabell "is more thorough in his art." [43] By 1927 Mencken was declaring that "Cabell came nearer being a first–rate artist than any American of his time."

Unlike the praise of Cabell, Mencken's tub-thumping for Dreiser can be read today without the same kind of "were-people-ever-like-that?" feeling. However, Mencken and the younger critics may have overvalued Dreiser as a pioneer. The twelve–year withdrawal of *Sister Carrie* from publication and the violent attacks by the critics of the establishment cast Dreiser in the role of martyr for the cause of literary freedom. As late as 1930 in his Nobel Prize address, Sinclair Lewis said:

> Now to me, as to many other American writers, Dreiser more than any other man, *marching alone* [ital. mine], usually unappreciated, and often hated, has cleared the trail from Victorian and Howellsian * timidity and gentility in American fiction to honesty and boldness and passion of life. Without his pioneer-ing, I doubt if any of us could, unless we went to jail, seek to express life and beauty and terror.[44]

* It should be recorded that Howells had been one of the first to hail Dreiser and the latter had praised Howells' *Their Wedding Journey*—"not a sentimental passage in it . . . quite beautiful and true." Clara M. and Rudolph Kirk, *William Dean Howells*, N. Y., 1962, p. 70.

This view of Dreiser as a lonely pioneer is reflected in Alfred Kazin's statement, "By exploding in the face of the Genteel Tradition, *Sister Carrie* made possible a new frankness in the American novel." [45] It would seem more accurate to say that *Sister Carrie* was part of a literary trend that had begun with *The Gilded Age* and included DeForest, Garland, Frederic, Crane, and Norris. Unlike Whitman, Dreiser did not break new ground nor create a new literary form. Nor was he the first to portray the Nietszchean type of business tycoon. His Frank Cowperwood was antedated by Harold Frederic's Joel Stormont Thorpe (*The Marketplace* 1899) and by Robert Herrick's E. V. Harrington (*The Memoirs of an American Citizen* 1905). Harrington's epiphany came when he served on the jury which convicted the Haymarket radicals:

> Suddenly a meaning of it all came to me like a great light. The strong must rule: the world was for the strong. It was the act of an idiot to deny the truth. . . . I saw it so then, and I have lived it so all my life.

Why then did Dreiser become such an important symbol during the second renaissance? Even his champion Mencken spoke of "the inescapable dullness of parts of *The Financier*" and "the general stupidity and stodginess of *The Genius*." [46] In fact all of the admirers of Dreiser deplored his heavy-handed style and his bad word-sense. And his sophomoric talk of "chemism" was only an embarrassment to his admirers. There was, of course, the undeniable force of the man despite all his artistic faults. He created some memorable characters; Carrie Meeber, Jennie Gerhardt, and Frank Cowperwood. Even so they remain rather slab-sided: one learns very early all about them as persons; only what will happen to them remains in doubt. Frederic's Joel Stormont Thorpe is a more complex superman than is Frank Cowperwood; the alleged artistic temperament of Dreiser's Eugene Witla expresses itself chiefly in the tireless pursuit of women; Carrie Meeber is from start to finish an amoral girl on the make. Only Jennie Gerhardt has real human warmth.

Much of the enthusiasm for Dreiser, it would appear, grew out of the anti-Puritan crusade of the era. Instead of being evaluated as a novelist he became a cause. For this, the critics representing the establishment were partly responsible. Their attacks on Dreiser were largely moralistic. As Mencken said with considerable justice, "What offends [Stuart Sherman] is not actually Dreiser's shortcomings as an artist, but Dreiser's shortcoming as a Christian and an American. . . ." [47] Mencken charged:

> Fully nine-tenths of the reviews of Dreiser's "The Titan," without question the best American novel of its year, were devoted chiefly to indignant denunciations of the morals of Frank Cowperwood. . . . They were Puritans writing for Puritans, and all they could see in Cowperwood was an anti-Puritan, and in its creator another. [48]

Mencken excoriated Howells and William Lyon Phelps for failing to recognize Dreiser:

> Search the latest volume of the Phelps revelation, "The Advance of the English Novel" and you will find that Dreiser is not once mentioned in it. The late O. Henry is hailed as a genius who will have "abiding fame" . . . and an obscure Pagliaccio named Charles D. Stewart is brought forward as "the American

novelist most worthy to fill the particular vacancy caused by the death of Mark Twain—but Dreiser is not even listed in the index.[49]

In his Nobel Prize address of 1930 Sinclair Lewis, in addition to praising Dreiser, presented a list which is a compendium of the literary dislikes and enthusiasms of the anti-Puritans. The villains included Howells, the New Humanists, the academic scholars, and the American Academy of Arts and Letters, a body in which Lewis listed Nicholas Murray Butler, Wilbur Cross, Edwin Arlington Robinson, Robert Frost, James Truslow Adams, Edith Wharton, Hamlin Garland, Owen Wister, Brand Whitlock, and Booth Tarkington. In Lewis's pantheon were Dreiser, O'Neill, Mencken, Masters, Randolph Bourne, Harriet Monroe, Millay, Sandburg, Jeffers, Lindsay, Cather, Hergesheimer, Sherwood Anderson, Louis Bromfield, Ring Lardner, Hemingway, Daniel Wilbur Steele, Fannie Hurst, Mary Austin, Cabell, Edna Ferber and Upton Sinclair.

Lewis, who was not much of an intellectual, was often a good reflecting mirror. His ideas tended to come from Mencken and other iconoclasts rather than from a trained literary sensibility. After all he was a refugee from the Yale of William Lyon Phelps.

Literary critics in all ages have made egregious mistakes about their contemporaries. In the days of Francis Jeffrey, Robert Southey, and Leigh Hunt the critics tended to praise or damn a writer on the basis of his political views. But between 1910 and 1930 the measuring stick was likely to be his commitment to or revolt from the Genteel Tradition which was confused with Puritanism.

As has been suggested, the iconoclasts as well as Howells overestimated the strength of that tradition on

American life and letters. As Emanie Sachs points out in her life of Victoria Woodhull: "The free-love movement, which had started in America in the Thirties was flourishing in 1870. It had its own preachers, its poets and its colonies. It published newspapers and organized excursions and picnics. All the papers were full of it." Nineteenth-century student diaries show that the conventions of courtship were far different from those represented in Howells' novels. An Amherst student of the 1840s on the basis of his experience with numerous respectable daughters of burghers and professors had in his diary described the various kinds of kisses he had experienced, including "the voluptuous kiss of love." Kissing games are referred to in Joel Barlow's *Hasty Pudding* and Whittier's *Snow Bound;* the song, "I Wonder Who's Kissing Her Now" (1909) was popular at a time when Howells was deploring the magazine-story kiss and embrace.

Obviously, literary conventions were often more squeamish than those of society. In 1884 Henry James remarked in *The Art of Fiction* that "In the English novel (by which of course I mean the American as well), more than in any other, there is a traditional difference between that which people know and that which they agree to admit that they know, that which they see and that which they speak of, and that which they feel to be a part of life and that which they allow to enter into literature. There is a great difference, in short, between what they talk of in conversation and what they talk of in print."

Earlier in this chapter, evidence was presented to show that despite the disapproval of the prudes, American novelists exercised a considerable latitude in dealing with supposedly forbidden topics. More important, the free-spoken books sold, often becoming best sellers. The Concord ban on *Huckleberry Finn* was an important force in pushing up its sales. Twain estimated that the ban would mean an additional sale of 25,000 copies.[50] In any case the book sold over 50,000 copies in its first three months.

As for Dreiser, Mencken's own evidence negates the claim that he was a neglected author. In a survey of public libraries in 1916 or '17 Mencken found Dreiser well represented.[51] New York had all but *Jennie Gerhardt* and *The Financier;* Chicago, Philadelphia, Kansas City, Newark, Denver, and Los Angeles had all the novels; only New Orleans and Providence had none. Boston, Hartford, and Baltimore carried only one or two of Dreiser's innocuous books. In 1912 the respected house of Harper took over the rights for *Sister Carrie* and re-issued it.

In 1915 Macmillan's brought out the volume of poetry which dominated the field until the appearance of Eliot's *The Waste Land.* This was Edgar Lee Masters' *Spoon River Anthology.* Mencken suggested that its great popularity was due to the notion that it was improper. The truth is that for thousands of Americans the book provided the shock of recognition: here was a realistic picture of a society many of them knew firsthand but had never quite looked at.

The most successful play of 1924 was *What Price Glory* by Lawrence Stallings and Maxwell Anderson—a ribald, realistic picture of soldiers at war. As Joseph Wood Krutch pointed out: "The great and instantaneous success of the play is itself proof of the fact that its moral assumptions were those of a large public ready to accept them. . . . This is reflected in the popular joke about two old ladies. At the end of the play one said, 'Shall we get the hell out of here?' To which the other answered 'Not till I find my goddam glasses.' " [52]

Nearly as successful that same year was Sidney Howard's *They Knew What They Wanted* wherein a

waitress wooed by a middle-aged Italian owner of a vine-
yard spends a night with a handsome young employee and
becomes pregnant. The boy runs away; the Italian marries
the girl. The boy wanted the girl; she wanted security;
and the Italian wanted a family. In a bitter-sweet manner
all of them got what they wanted. Here again as Krutch
says, this play like *What Price Glory* demonstrates "the
fact that native dramatists were coming to assume the
possibility of taking for granted in their audience moral
attitudes which were still being described as advanced." [53]

In fact the often spectacular success of nongenteel
writing from George Lippard, Mark Twain, Harold
Frederic, Stephen Crane, and Upton Sinclair to Edgar
Lee Masters, Sinclair Lewis, Lawrence Stallings, and Maxwell Anderson is a refutation of the reiterated claim that
the Puritan had sealed the lips of American writers. Certainly some of the distaste for Dreiser was due as much
to his tediousness as to his subject matter.

Prudes and Puritans there undoubtedly were, but the
iconoclasts were obviously wrong in regarding these as
exclusively American types. They were equally the targets
of Shaw, Ibsen, and D. H. Lawrence. Mencken came closer
to the mark in damning the professors. Especially in English departments they were part of a literary establishment
which kept its opera glass trained on England. Some of
them shared the view of Barrett Wendell who in *The
Literary History of America* said:

> The American Revolution, then, disuniting the
> English-speaking race, has had on history an effect
> which those who cherish the moral and political herit-
> age of our language may well grow to feel in some
> degree tragic.[54]

At Saint Paul's School, that training ground for the Ivy League colleges, the only game permitted by the headmaster, Dr. Coit, was cricket.

Certainly the establishment's ideas of what was meet and proper tended to reflect current Victorian standards. Thus when Richard Watson Gilder changed certain colloquial expressions in *Huckleberry Finn* before printing an excerpt in the *Century* he was in accord with Matthew Arnold's view of prose style—the Arnold who criticized General Grant for writing "an English without charm or high breeding." [55] It is significant that at a later date Grant's prose was praised by such diverse persons as Howells and Gertrude Stein, and that in 1966 Justin Kaplan could say, ". . . today the book seems as remarkable as ever for its muscular directness and its avoidance of chest-thumping and martial rhetoric." [56]

It was muscular directness which offended the establishment. Thus Howells, in going over proofs for *The Prince and the Pauper,* suggested the deletion of such words as *devil, hick,* and *basting.*[57] Gilder, editing selections from *Huckleberry Finn* for the *Century,* deleted references to nakedness, blasphemy, smells, and dead cats; he changed "in a sweat" to "worrying." [58] Dreiser complained that Doubleday, Page and Co., the first publishers of *Sister Carrie,* objected to such usages as *vest* for *waistcoat.* It is the same sort of finicky propriety that on both sides of the Atlantic caused "legs" to be called "limbs" and produced the British euphemism *Little Mary* for *stomach*—the coy title of a play by Barrie.

There was an element of Puritanism in this sort of thing of course, but there was more than a little pedantry. For at least a hundred years college professors had argued that a thorough knowledge of Latin was the best foundation for good English. As Bonamy Dobree demonstrated, the published prose of English writers like Matthew Arnold was far different from the colloquial style of their letters. This is what Hemingway was talking about when he said that modern literature began with *Huckleberry Finn*. Frost argued that the rhythms of actual speech were important in conveying the meaning of a poem. In a review of Paul Shorey's *The Assault on Humanism* (1917) Randolph Bourne attacked the notion of Latin as the basis for good English:

> No American thought, criticism, or literary art of any creative value whatever comes from these guardians of the classical tradition, who are given to expressing themselves with an incoherence of thought and an insensitiveness to style that we should complain of in modern journalism.[59]

It was a problem Henry James never solved. He included colloquialisms, even slang—often apologetically—in some of the most pedantic prose in fiction. American publishers long continued the use of British spellings like *colour* and *parlour*. Van Wyck Brooks or his publishers always used them. Edith Wharton, who boasted that she had been taught correct—not American—English, railed against such supposedly barbarous usages as *gotten* and *guess* (to mean suppose). Members of the establishment were seldom aware that these were survivals of Shakespearian English.

One reason that Mark Twain had been able to break new ground in the use of colloquial American English was that he published his books in the subscription press, that is through publishers whose salesmen took orders from door to door. He did this not in order to escape the restrictions of conservative editors but simply because he

thought he could make more money. It was a less dignified
form of publication and to a considerable degree hindered
his recognition as a literary artist. The unsophisticated
public who patronized the subscription publishers was less
squeamish than the Anglophile editors, critics, and professors of literature.

It is even possible that some of the hostility on the
part of the establishment to writers like Dreiser, Masters,
Anderson, and Lewis was due less to Puritanism than to a
snobbish distaste for the kinds of people they chose to
write about. Walter Hines Page, the senior partner of
Doubleday, Page and Co. wrote to Dreiser in 1900, saying
that the choice of characters in *Sister Carrie* was unfortunate. "I think I told you personally, this kind of people
do not interest me and we find it hard to believe they will
interest the great majority of readers." [60]

A hundred years before, this sort of distaste characterized the attacks on Wordsworth's representation of
peasants and peddlers. The aristocratic Byron sneered at
"these Jack Cades of sense and song." Certainly this kind
of attitude is reflected in Barrett Wendell's remarks on
Whitman and *Huckleberry Finn,* and in Gilder's censor-
ship of Twain's vernacular. Irving Babbitt's comment on
Lewis reveals the aristocratic distaste of a critic who
regarded the age of Louis XIV as the pinnacle of what he
called decorum: "According to the author of 'Main Street'
the average is not divine but trivial; according to the
author of 'Spoon River Anthology,' it is positively hide-
ous." [61] Stuart Sherman found modern literature lacking
in the values of the English gentleman and the Southern
cavalier.

The opponents of Puritanism who often shared
aristocratic sentiments, agreed in linking it to an emphasis
on the commercial virtues of thrift, industry, and tem-

perance. For this emphasis there were sound sociological and economic reasons. An overwhelming proportion of the people who had settled in America, whether Puritans or pagans, were small farmers, artisans, and laborers. For these classes hard work and sobriety were necessities for survival. The maxims of the far-from-Puritan Poor Richard were merely common sense. Early to bed and keep your shop were not ideological propositions; they were the economic facts of life. Certainly there were unlovely aspects of such doctrines; they left small room for aesthetic values.*

These lower-middle-class values had for economic reasons taken root in the Middle West. The Spoon Rivers, Winesburgs, Gopher Prairies and growing Zeniths had been settled by people who had to work for a living; there was at first an almost entire absence of inherited wealth. Also these farmers, artisans, and store keepers, whether native, German, or Scandinavian lacked the tradition of learning which had existed in New England from the beginning. Perry Miller estimated that in the early days of the Puritan settlement there were more Cambridge men in Massachusetts than in any county in England outside of London. With all its faults Brahmin Boston tended to maintain the real Puritan values—an emphasis on things of the mind and spirit.

Therefore the rebels against village values were largely mistaken in treating them as the heritage of New England Puritanism. It is worth noting that Dreiser represented Carrie Meeber's Swedish brother-in-law as

---

* The really surprising thing is the number of painters, sculptors, writers and scholars produced by these farmers, artisans, and business men. To mention a few there were Franklin, Copley, Irving, West, Thoreau, Hawthorne, Ticknor, Bancroft, Greenough, Morse, Whittier, Whitman, Twain, Emily Dickinson, Longfellow, Howells, Willa Cather, Lewis, Fitzgerald—the list is endless.

narrowly puritanical; so did Willa Cather with the Scandinavian parents of Thea Kronberg. For that matter it was an Irish Catholic Boston which made possible the suppression of books by the Watch and Ward Society. In the twentieth century Cotton Mather and Jonathan Edwards, those bêtes noires of William Carlos Williams, were less influential than Saint Patrick. Bishop Cannon, the patron saint of the prohibitionists, was not the heir of the hard-drinking seventeenth-century Puritans but of John Wesley, apostle to the working classes—victims of low wages and cheap gin.

Obviously the catch-all term *Puritan* so much used by the iconoclasts was a vast oversimplification of complex historical, economic and social forces. An Anglophile literary and academic establishment and a lower middle class concerned with thrift, industry, and temperance were operating from different corners of the field. The Irish-Americans, who hated Prohibition, were puritanical about sex. The Transcendentalists, so abused by the anti-Puritans, were in fact the direct ancestors of Whitman, John Dewey and Martin Luther King.

In their war against Puritanism the iconoclasts reflected the social changes which had been accelerating since the 1890s. What was happening was that the United States was shifting from a rural to an urban culture, an urban culture made up of many races and drawing its literary inspiration from all of Europe. The cultural dependence upon England which had characterized the literary and academic establishment was passing. Beginning with Howells, Crane, and Norris, writers discovered Tolstoy, Flaubert, Zola, Dostoevsky, and Chekhov. The pioneering role of James Gibbon Huneker in this discovery has already been mentioned. In many ways his was the first great critical voice of cosmopolitan America.

However it is easy to overestimate the influence of literature in the shift from provincial to cosmopolitan viewpoints. The trek of boys and girls to the city was part of it. This physical and psychic migration is reflected in much of the fiction of the period, the odysseys and *bildungsromans* of young people leaving a village or provincial town for Chicago, New York or Europe. The theme appears in Cather's *Song of the Lark* and *Youth and the Bright Medusa,* in Dell's *The Moon Calf,* Dreiser's *The Genius* and *Sister Carrie,* Van Vechten's *The Tattooed Countess* and Wolfe's *Look Homeward, Angel.* Anderson's *Winesburg, Ohio* ends with George Willard's departure for the city. Tom Little, the railway conductor, makes no comment as he punches George's ticket:

> Tom had seen a thousand George Willard's go out of their towns to the city.

By 1912 Greenwich Village was filled with refugees from the provinces—young people seeking freedom in art and sex.

Less obvious and more difficult to document was a rapid change in mores. As so often happens, these filtered down from the wealthy and sophisticated to the middle classes. Thomas Beers' *The Mauve Decade* shows that as early as the 1890s a considerable amount of hedonism had appeared in American society. So too does Ralph Martin's *Jennie,* the biography of the wealthy American girl who married Randolph Churchill. In upper-class circles women had begun to smoke cigarettes. Edith Wharton's *The House of Mirth* (1905) gives a similar picture of New York society. It was a class which spent much time in Europe and like Mrs. Jack Gardner brought back not only works of art but European attitudes. The more sensational activities of the wealthy were widely publicized by the yellow press. A middle-class public, which might be shocked by Dreiser, avidly read the newspaper stories about Harry Thaw, Evelyn Nesbit and Stanford White. Before America entered World War I, Fitzgerald's Amory Blaine on a tour with a Triangle show discovered that the petting party was an established institution in all parts of the country.

All this helps to explain why a large public so quickly accepted a literature critical of Puritanism. In 1924 Mencken remarked about recent books:

> Today at least half which reach me deal with sex in a bold and often scandalous manner and some of the worst are published by the most respectable Barabbases in the business. . . .[62]
>
> I have seen things in the *Century* and the *Atlantic* during the past six months that would have caused a shock, twenty years ago, in the *Police Gazette*.

Similarly Sherwood Anderson, who in 1920 was complaining about the attacks on the morality of *Winesburg, Ohio*, wrote in 1922: [63]

> And in my own time I was to see the grip of the old New England, the Puritanic culture, begin to loosen. A physical incoming of the Celts, Slavs, men of the Far East, the blood of the dreaming nations of the world gradually flowing thicker and thicker in the body of America, and the shrewd shop-keeping money-saving blood of the northern men getting thinner and thinner.[64]

Thus Anderson, while recognizing the changed climate of opinion, was still echoing the clichés of the period: that Puritanism was a New England heritage; that it was a money-grubbing philosophy, and that Europeans were more idealistic than old-stock Americans. Like so many of his contemporaries he misread American history and misunderstood the social revolution he was living through. The urbanization and industrialization which he, like other intellectuals so much hated, were the very forces which were destroying the village values of hard work, thrift, total abstinence, orthodoxy, fundamentalism, and sexual repression—the values which the iconoclasts called Puritan.

All of the foregoing discussion suggests that the writers and critics between 1910 and 1930—especially after 1920—were conducting a mopping-up operation against enemies already on the run. After all, Howells died in 1920. Since the 1880s a considerable number of novelists had worked outside the genteel tradition. Huneker was more urbane than Mencken, the early Brooks, Waldo Frank or William Carlos Williams. The enthusiasm with which the reading public accepted *Spoon River* and *Main Street* shows that a large number of people questioned the old village values. The old literary establishment against which Lewis was still tilting in 1930 was fighting a rearguard action.

As Krutch said apropos of drama:

> A good deal of the talk which lingered, even during the twenties, about "daring ideas" was no more than cant since it had long ceased to require any particular courage to question either the social or the moral code. *Attacks on "puritanism" were about as safe as*

attacks upon "snobbery" had been during the Victorian era. [Ital. mine] [65]

The writers of the second renaissance did create certain enduring myths about American culture and literature. By inflating the image of the Puritan bogeyman they were able to represent our society as uniquely repressive and sterile; by harping on this theme they were able to pose as daring crusaders.

3.

The Pillared Portico

The most concerted attempt at a counterrevolution against the trends in contemporary literature came from a group of critics—largely Anglophile and academic—who called themselves the New Humanists. The leaders were Paul Elmer More of Princeton, Irving Babbitt of Harvard, Stuart Sherman of the University of Iowa, and Norman Foerster of the University of North Carolina. All had studied at Harvard and directly or indirectly they were heirs of the Anglophile and antidemocratic tradition of Charles Eliot Norton and Barrett Wendell.

Despite the fact that More left teaching to become editor of *The Nation* between 1909 and 1914, his writing never lost a donnish quality. For twenty years after he left *The Nation* he lectured at Princeton. His fourteen volumes of *Shelburne Essays,* begun in 1904, contain much of the best literary criticism written by any of the New Humanists, but like the others he was hostile to modern literature. Babbitt, who taught French literature (which

he hated) at Harvard, began his series of diatribes against
Rousseau, humanitarianism, modern education, and modern literature in 1908 with *Literature and the American
College.* Then came *The New Laöckoon* in 1910, *Rousseau
and Romanticism,* 1919; *Democracy and Leadership,* 1924.
Sherman, who wrote book reviews for *The Nation,* published *On Contemporary Literature* (1917), *The Genius
of America* (1923) and *The Emotional Discovery of
America* (1932). Originally very hostile to the realists he
gradually moved away from the other New Humanists far
enough to praise a few modern writers.

These men achieved a certain prominence when they
were attacked by Mencken and his followers. But their
heyday came in 1928 with a series of articles on Humanism
in *Forum* magazine and with the publication of several
books: Gorham B. Munson's *Destinations:* Norman Foerster's *American Criticism;* and More's *The Demon of the
Absolute.*[1] For two or three years there was a spate of
books and articles pro and con. In particular *The Bookman*
under Seward Collins became a forum for New Humanist
criticism.

The noisy war between Mencken and the New
Humanists tended to obscure the fact that both sides
shared a basic premise—the theory that democracy and
culture were incompatible. These writers were more concerned with social than with political democracy. Insofar
as they considered political ideas it was to reject everything
from the Declaration of Independence to the social legislation of the Progressive era. Their political views will
be considered later; this chapter will be concerned chiefly
with their attempt to evaluate literature and culture
according to aristocratic principles.

Despite the shared premise that democracy was hostile
to culture, the two warring groups diverged sharply on

other fundamentals. Mencken and his followers were vehemently anti-Puritan; the New Humanists were authoritarian in morals. In fact they might be more accurately termed the Neo-Puritans. For instance, More on reading that Longfellow had written only one love poem could "honour him for his reserve." Somewhat myopically he could detect in Poe "no single spot where the abnormal sinks to the unclean." As for the moderns "The only form of literature to-day wherein you may be sure the author will not play tricks with the Ten Commandments is the detective story." [2]

It was this Puritan element in New Humanists' criticism which kept them out of the mainstream of the second American renaissance before the emergence of Eliot; it was their basic assumptions about the aristocratic nature of true culture and about the need for authority which made their doctrines an important force in the late 1920s.

To grossly oversimplify the situation one might say that American literature of the first thirty or forty years of this century divided into two main channels: one flowing from Jefferson, Emerson, and Whitman; the other from the courtly muses of Europe by way of the Ivy League colleges. The first became contaminated by Leninism and Stalinism, the second by fascism and racism. But this is to get ahead of the story.

It is one of the ironies of literary history that the neo-Puritanism of More, Babbitt, Foerster, and Sherman led directly to the neo-Thomism of T. S. Eliot. But perhaps the confluence was not accidental. Psychologically at least, the New Humanists and the neo-Thomists were authoritarian in religion, politics, and literary criticism; and they tended to equate sex with sin.

Thus More seemed to find Michael Wigglesworth and Jonathan Edwards more congenial thinkers than Cooper, James or Twain; he omitted Melville entirely. After quoting Wigglesworth on the pains of hell More added:

> Say what you will, there is a grim sincerity in these lines which lifts them out of the commonplace and gives them something of the ring of poetry; and after all, if you are going to depict an eternal hell, there is no use in being finicky about the benevolence of your deity.[3]

Commenting on the assignment of children who died in infancy to "the easiest room in hell," More wrote, "Wigglesworth spoke the honest and deep-rooted conviction of his contemporaries—and they were not mad." [4] This is the crux of the issue: the opponents of More, Babbitt and Sherman felt that men such as Wigglesworth, Cotton Mather, and Jonathan Edwards who would condemn most of mankind to eternal fire were mad—as a later generation of liberals thought that Hitler, Himmler, and Goebbels were mad. Thus for William Carlos Williams the books of Cotton Mather ". . . are a vessel that vomits up a thing that obsesses my quiet, that allows no tranquility, a broken, a maimed, a foul thing—that they tell me is sweet, PURE." [5]

The extent to which theology got confused with literary criticism is shown not only in More's praise of the jingling verse of Michael Wigglesworth but in his views on Jonathan Edwards. Referring to Edwards' call for disciplining young sinners who read such novels as *Pamela,* More remarked ". . . we may admire the literary taste of youthful Northampton, yet think that their pastor

was justified in condemning such reading as incendiary."
He equated the excesses of Edwards' sermons on hell with
the literature of the Romantic movement:

> Often the reader of these treatises is struck by a
> curious, and by no means accidental resemblance
> between the position of Edwards and the position of
> the apologists of the romantic movement in literature.
> There is the same directness of appeal to the emo-
> tions, the same laudation of expansiveness, at the
> cost, if need be, of judgment or measure or other
> restraint.[6]

One wonders if the work of Scott, Wordsworth,
Coleridge, Byron, Shelley, or Keats ever had the effect of
Edwards' sermons which caused some of his congregation
to commit suicide or go mad.

Nevertheless More argued that Edwards never "in any
proper sense of the word, lapsed from the virtue of
Christian humility." This of the man who wrote:

> . . . when I ask for humility, I cannot bear the
> thought of being no more humble than other Chris-
> tians. It seems to me, that though their degrees of
> humility may be suitable for them, yet it would be a
> vile self-exaltation to me, not to be the lowest in
> humility of all mankind.

This humble Christian followed Saint Thomas Aquinas
in picturing the damned "tormented in the presence of
the holy angels, and in the presence of the Lamb, and
when you shall be in this state of suffering, the glorious
inhabitants of heaven shall go forth and look on the awful
spectacle, that they may see what the wrath and fierceness

of the Almighty is; and when they have seen it, they will fall down and adore that great power and majesty."

But for More, "Northampton has the distinction of having rejected the greatest theologian and philosopher yet produced in this country." [7] Another of the New Humanists, Norman Foerster would have agreed. Years later he wrote: "The last and greatest Puritan, Jonathan Edwards, had perhaps the finest intellect America has produced." [8] This admiration for abstract thought and ingenious logic-chopping ignores the real humanistic large-mindedness of men like Franklin, Jefferson, Madison, Emerson, Thoreau, and Justice Holmes.

The preference for Edwards over the great democratic thinkers is not accidental. Ignoring the fact that aristocracies have rarely excelled in the exercise of Puritanical ideals, the New Humanists pictured the Tories of the world as guardians of standards of conduct and literature. For More the true critics were "discriminators between the false and the true, the deformed and the normal; preachers of harmony and proportion and order. . . ." [9] Therefore they "stand with the great conservative forces of human nature [Ital. mine], having their fame certified by the things that endure amid all the betrayals of time and fashion."

In an appreciative essay on More by Stuart Sherman, written when he was tenting with the New Humanists, literary standards were specifically linked to moral and aristocratic virtues:

The Tories are always right—more often right, perhaps, than their adversaries, because they shun experiment and settle back into the easy chair of experience, and build solidly and stolidly on the experiments of the radicals of other days. Mr. More is indubitably

right when he insists that most of us think we are
better than we are; that we need a new sense of sin,
that we need the idea of God; that organized society
is impossible without a stern discrimination of values
. . . that the leadership of superior men is an ever-
lasting necessity; and that women are, in many
respects, a whimsical and troublesome sex, and have
led us into much mischief.[10]

By "superior men" Sherman was almost certainly not
thinking of Jefferson's natural aristocracy of talent but of
a traditional upper class such as the English university
man of the nineteenth century, whom he described thus:

He knew what he was there for. . . . He knew that it
was his business to produce a Christian, a scholar, and
a gentleman. . . . No finished product has been made
in modern times without the use of these three molds;
and we Americans have discarded them one by one,
most completely in the west, and in the typical educational institutions of the west, the State Universities. . . .[11]

For Sherman the two great types of character produced in
America were:

the New England Puritan and the southern Cavalier—
the gentleman of the Old South. These two types were
produced mainly under two great formative forces:
the formative force of religion and the formative force
of an aristocratic society. But these two great types
are gone. When John Quincy Adams was beaten at
the polls by Andrew Jackson, the doom of the Puritan

was sounded. When Robert E. Lee surrendered to
Grant at Appomattox the doom of the Cavalier was
sounded. The triumph of the western rabble
began. . . .[12]

This "western rabble" that he was talking of included
such writers as Garland, Herrick, Dreiser, Hecht, Sherwood
Anderson, Sandburg, Masters, and Lewis. Sherman's semi-
mythical Cavalier before the Civil War produced almost
no literature, nor did he invariably behave as a gentleman.
The Harvard and Göttington scholar, James Cogswell, who
went to teach at the University of South Carolina in the
1840s, found that he had to make the sons of Southern
planters take off their hats in class, and Congressman
Charles Sumner, the victim of a brutal beating by a
Cavalier senator, noted that in Europe the Southern
planters were chiefly distinguished for tobacco-chewing
and bad manners. Faulkner in *The Bear,* by means of
old ledgers, represents antebellum plantation owners in
Mississippi as nearly illiterate. Sherman, like others of his
kind who pictured Jackson as the leader of an uncouth
mob, forgot that the Jacksonians included Cooper, Irving
(for a time), Hawthorne, Bryant, Horatio Greenough,
Bancroft, and Whitman, a number of whom were enter-
tained by Jackson at the White House. In fact Jackson
after his antinullification speech became much more of
a hero to the Brahmin Puritans than to the slave-owning
Cavaliers. Harvard gave him an honorary degree.[13]
Just as the young iconoclasts had developed the
doctrinaire image of the Puritan, the conservatives whether
New Humanist or Menckenite, created the mythical
Cavalier—an image that became a stereotype in the hands
of "The Fugitive" group during the 1930s. The foregoing

comments may seem to have little to do with literary values, but the point is that much of the criticism of the second American renaissance was concerned with these ethical, sociological, and pseudo-historical matters.

Paul Elmer More frankly admitted his inability to judge the artistic qualities of literature: "If you should ask me by what rhetorical devices or by what instrument of representation one poem or work of art appeals more successfully than another to the higher faculty within us . . . though both poems were written with equally good intentions, I would reply frankly that the solution of this problem is beyond my powers of critical analysis." [14]

For Babbitt a work was damned if it contained a trace of either Rousseau or humanitarianism. Not only did all the writers of the Romantic movement come under Babbitt's anathema, so too did many other people, including Jefferson, Jackson, Whitman, Charles W. Eliot, Woodrow Wilson, John Dewey, and the naturalists whether French, Russian, or American. Babbitt, who argued for "the law of measure" in others, said however that "When first principles are involved the law of measure is no longer applicable. One should not be moderate in dealing with error." [15] As Edmund Wilson has pointed out, "Professor Babbitt, in his writings is always engaged in 'dealing with error.' " [16]

Although Babbitt did not often use the term *aristocracy* he tended to use *democracy* as an epithet: "One is inclined, indeed, to ask . . . whether in this country in particular we are not in danger of producing in the name of democracy one of the most trifling brands of the human species that the world has yet seen." He quoted with approval *Punch's* remark that the United States was not a country but a picnic. Universal suffrage was dangerous because it endangered the "safety for the institution of property that genuine justice and genuine civilization both require."

The point here is not the reactionary nature of Babbitt's social and political views, but that like his enemy Mencken he evaluated literature almost exclusively in terms of his doctrinaire opinions. Mencken gave lip service to the idea that the critic should be a catalytic agent between the writer and the reader, but his practice is better described by his title *Prejudices*. Babbitt was more honest when asked by Edmond Scherer if criticism did not consist above all in comprehending; Babbitt answered, "No, but in judging." [17] For Babbitt this did not mean an impartial judicial function but the sentencing of criminals for guilt by association with Rousseau.

This sometimes led him into tortured reasoning and too often into distortions of the evidence. Thus he blamed laws like Prohibition on Jeffersonianism. "The inner check upon the expansion of natural impulse is precisely the missing element in the Jeffersonian philosophy. The Jeffersonian has therefore been led to deal with the problem of evil, not vitally in terms of the inner life, but mechanically." [18] This ignored not only Jefferson's life-long insistence on the need for private judgment rather than external authority, but also the fact that many of the opponents to Prohibition based their arguments on Jeffersonian principles.

In a similar way Babbitt distorted the views of Walt Whitman whom he accused of not admitting "the need of the leader who looks up humbly to some standard and so becomes worthy to be looked up to in turn." [19] This of the man who in his poem on Lincoln called him "the sweetest, wisest soul of all my days and lands," and who in *Passage to India* and *Democratic Vistas* called for the poet who shall bring the spiritual vision to unite a world now only physically united by the work of engineers and scientists: "The true son of God shall absolutely fuse them." But for Babbitt, Whitman's idea of a leader "represents in an extreme form the substitution for vital control of expansive emotion under the name of love." [20] Babbitt preferred a leader like Mussolini.

Babbitt even undertook to interpret the New Testament in accord with his political and social opinions. "I have sought to show," he wrote "that humanitarian service cannot . . . be properly derived from Christ." [21] The idea of "service" was not Christian because "the Christian serves not man but God." Apparently Babbitt chose to disregard the sermon on the mount in which Jesus said that the service of God was feeding the hungry, giving drink to the thirsty, clothing the naked, visiting the sick, and housing the stranger.

Using the technique of More and Babbitt, Mencken in discussing American literature scissored it to fit his own social theories. He saw America from its beginnings as "a commonwealth of peasants and small traders, a paradise of the third rate, and its national philosophy unchecked by the more sophisticated and civilized ideas of an aristocracy." [22] In 1920 he wrote:

> The native culture of the country—that is, the culture of the low caste Anglo-Saxons who preserve the national tradition—is almost completely incapable of producing ideas. It is a culture that roughly corresponds to what the culture of England would be if there were no universities over there, and no caste of individualists and no landed aristocracy . . . the United States has not yet produced anything properly describable as an aristocracy, and so there is no impediment to the domination of the inferior orders. [23]

Given these premises certain conclusions naturally followed, one of them being that New England writers were rather mediocre. The only true civilization in America had been that of the antebellum South:

I say a civilization because that is what, in the old days, the South had, despite the Baptist and Methodist barbarism that reigns down there now. More, it was a civilization of manifold excellences—perhaps the best that the Western Hemisphere has ever seen— undoubtedly the best that these States have ever seen. Down to the middle of the last century, and even beyond, the main hatchery of ideas on this side of the water was across the Potomac bridges. The New England shopkeepers and theologians never really developed a civilization: all they developed was a government.[24]

This interesting view of America's intellectual history to 1861 was accompanied by sociological and genetic theories resting on an equally sound foundation of scholarship. Mencken's explanation for "The Sahara of the Bozart," [25] as he described the South of 1920, was that the old aristocracy had taken Negro mistresses instead of improving the breed of the lower classes of whites as European aristocrats had always done. Therefore when the lower orders came into power in the new South, they were a biologically inferior class. This largely explained why "it is almost as sterile, artistically, intellectually, culturally, as the Sahara Desert."

For Mencken the one oasis in this cultural wasteland was the work of James Branch Cabell, who had the advantage of being both anti-Puritan and an aristocrat. "For such a pure Anglo-Saxon as Cabell to disport himself in the field of ideas is a rarity in the United States—and no exception to the rule that I have just mentioned, for Cabell belongs to an aristocracy that is now almost extinct. . . ." [26] As has been noted Mencken argued that Cabell came nearer being a first rate artist than any American of his time.

Cabell himself ridiculed "the excessive claims of democracy, which is the form of government chosen by the devils. . . ." [27] Like More, Babbitt, and Mencken, he paraded his distaste for humanitarianism: "I burn with generous indignation over this world's pig-headedness and injustice at no time whatever." [28] Like so much of the literary criticism of the era Cabell's was influenced by his political and social views. Thus in a discussion of Joseph Hergesheimer he concluded by saying, "America has produced, and is even nourishing, a literary artist of the first rank. Which is absurd of course, and a contention not to be supported this side of Bedlam, and, none the less, is my firm private belief." [29] Cabell may have been familiar with Hergesheimer's remark that giving money to starving children in Europe was "one of the least engaging ways in which money could be spent." Mencken had similar views: he argued that the Negro had been better off under slavery, and that the steel worker with his twelve-hour day was drunken, bawdy, and happy. The proponents of aristocracy rarely cited the principle of *noblesse oblige.* They belonged to the let-them-eat-cake school of thought.

A corollary to the doctrine that culture was an aristocratic monopoly was the opinion that anything popular was necessarily vulgar. Thus for Mencken "The jazz-band fetches only vulgarians, barbarians, idiots, pigs." [30] Similarly Irving Babbitt coupled Charlie Chaplin with Billy Sunday and Harold Bell Wright as examples of the vulgar idols of the American public.[31] What must foreign critics think of such a people? Neither Mencken nor Babbitt seemed to be aware that jazz music and Charlie Chaplin were both taken seriously by European sophisticates. In the lively arts as in literature the young radicals showed more aesthetic awareness than did the authoritarians. In *Vanity Fair* Edmund Wilson, Gilbert Seldes, John Peale Bishop, Carl Van Vechten, and Virgil Thomson all wrote studies of American jazz.[32]

Mencken ridiculed Van Vechten's enthusiasm for Schoenberg and Strawinsky [sic]—what Mencken called "the powerful shiverings and tremblings of M. Strawinsky. . . ." "The simple truth is that the accentuation of mere rhythm is a proof not of progress in music, but of a reversion to barbarism. . . . The African savage, beating his tom-tom, is content to go no further; the American composer of fox trots is with him." [33]

Allied to this penchant for regarding anything popular as barbarous was a tendency to judge writers by their social origins or even by their standing as WASPs. Thus Paul Elmer More damned a school of American fiction partly because its leading members were "almost without exception from small towns sprinkled along the Mid-Western states from Ohio to Kansas . . . self-made men with no *inherited background of culture*." [Ital. mine] [34] Stuart Sherman described Dreiser as a "barbaric naturalist" and charged that the younger generation was following "alien guides." [35] On another occasion he called Mencken pro-German.[36] He hailed *Main Street* for rescuing American literature from malign foreign influences:

> From the "lunatic fringe" of experimentation there was an ominous buzzing of "Freudians." Whatever was most unwholesome in the fiction of Russia,

> France, Germany, and the younger England was cried
> up by our criticasters and seized upon for imita-
> tion. . . . But in the fall of 1920 arrived, to deliver
> the beleaguered citadel of our hope and sanity, Mr.
> Sinclair Lewis and *Main Street*.[37]

As Ludwig Lewisohn said, the jibe that Stuart Sherman
was practicing Ku Klux Klan criticism was essentially
correct.[38] Mencken, never a very reliable witness, may
have had a point when he argued that xenophobia was
a big factor in the dislike of writers with foreign names
like Dreiser, Oppenheimer, etc.[39] A disciple of More's,
Seward Collins, who as editor of *The Bookman* championed the New Humanists, charged that some prominent
American writers were "the sons of recent arrivals in this
country." [40]

Mencken reversed the coin by arguing that culture
was chiefly a European product, that "the Anglo-Saxon
strain, second-rate at the start, has tended to degenerate
steadily to lower levels—in New England very markedly." [41]
Mencken was of course right in pointing out the great
contribution to American science by such continental
Jews as Flexner, Loeb, and Carrel. But he went overboard
in arguing that "an air of foreignness" clings to excep-
tional American compositions. It accounted for "the sur-
prise which must inevitably seize upon anyone who en-
counters a decent piece of writing in so vast a desert
of mere literacy. The native author of any genuine force
and originality is almost invariably found to be under
strong foreign influences. . . ." [42] So, too, of course, were
Chaucer, Shakespeare, Spenser, Milton, Fielding, Browning, Arnold, Shaw, or almost anyone who could be named.
Freneau, born in America and a graduate of Princeton,

was, according to Mencken, "thoroughly French in blood and traditions" [43]—a statement which completely disregarded Freneau's own citations of his favorites: Homer, Vergil, Dryden, Milton, Pope, and Macpherson—a list that includes not one French writer. Mencken even found an air of foreignness in such thoroughly American stories as Crane's *The Blue Hotel* and Edith Wharton's *Ethan Frome,* because they escaped the "superficiality of the inferior man . . . the chief hallmark of the American novel." [44] If a work was superior, it was not American.

Mencken's literary criticism like that of the New Humanists and the early Brooks was chiefly a brief for the prosecution against American culture. Brooks once spoke of the "absentee-mindedness" of More and Babbitt; he could with almost equal justice apply the epithet to Mencken or to his own early work. Recalling in later life his mood of 1920 Brooks wrote, "It took me twenty years or more to live down what I felt then, a frequent homesickness for the European scene. . . ." [45]

This absentee-mindedness appears in Brooks' often repeated charge that America lacked an "organic native culture." He spoke of "the vicious circle in which we revolve. In the absence both of an intellectual tradition and a sympathetic soil, we who above all peoples need great men and great ideals have been unable to develop the latent greatness we possess. . . ." It is to be feared that Brooks, like his contemporaries More, Babbitt, and Mencken, was thinking of culture and tradition in aristocratic terms. This is clearly implied in his account of his belated discovery of American folk-culture.

However Brooks never adopted the snobbish tone of Mencken and the New Humanists, that of an aristocrat putting the peasants in their place. Nor did he preach an authoritarian gospel of the negative virtues. But as has been shown, his social theories often led him to dubious critical judgments.

The tendency to judge literature in terms of one's social and political predilections appears also in the critical writing of T. S. Eliot. In 1920 he argued that honest criticism should be directed not upon the poet but upon the poetry. The mature poet did not necessarily have a more interesting mind nor have more to say than the immature poet; rather he had "a more finely perfected medium"—in other words was a finer artist.[46] However by 1934 Eliot was arguing that "Literary criticism should be completed by criticism from a definite ethical and theological standpoint. . . . In ages like our own, in which there is no . . . common agreement, it is the more necessary for Christian readers to scrutinize their reading, especially of works of the imagination, with explicit ethical and theological standards." [47]

In this connection it is worth noting that the writers whose techniques Eliot deplored were almost invariably those whose views on religion, society, and politics conflicted with his own: Milton, Blake, Byron, Shelley, Whitman, D. H. Lawrence; whereas those he praised such as Dante, Donne, Dryden, Kipling, and Pound were orthodox or reactionary in religion and politics. Arguing that "Dante made great poetry out of a great philosophy of life; and Shakespeare made equally great poetry out of an inferior and muddled philosophy of life" Eliot went on to undercut Shakespeare: *Hamlet* is "most certainly an artistic failure" [48] and Thomas Rymer, the seventeenth-century critic who called *Othello* a bloody farce, "makes a very good case."

In many ways Eliot never outgrew the teachings of his former professor, Irving Babbitt. Like others of the reactionary critics Eliot reconstituted cultural history in aristocratic terms. Addressing the believer in political equality he wrote ". . . if it seems monstrous to him that anyone should have the advantage of birth—I do not ask him to change his faith. I merely ask him to stop paying lip service to culture." Now unless *culture* means chiefly an Oxbridge accent or unless the "advantage of birth" means a middle-class origin, that statement is nonsense. In almost every era the leisure classes have been the consumers—not the producers of art and literature. In the long history of English literature only one major writer, Lord Byron, belonged to the nobility. The conferring of a title, as on Sir Thomas Browne or Alfred Lord Tennyson, is not the same thing as Eliot's "the advantage of birth." It is, of course, this kind of literary snobbery which is back of the search for an aristocratic author for Shakespeare's plays.

This doctrine that literature and art were an aristocratic monopoly was basic to the argument that America had no culture, a contention stemming from Henry James and embracing such disparate writers as Brooks (in his early period), Waldo Frank, Paul Elmer More, Irving Babbitt, H. L. Mencken, James Branch Cabell (cf. his comment on Hergesheimer), Ezra Pound, William Carlos Williams, and T. S. Eliot. In variant forms this article of faith held on for half a century. As late as 1955 Leslie Fiedler could say, "Like most American writers, Fitzgerald had to work without an accepted tradition to sustain him or received standards against which to measure himself." *Received standards* has a nice British ring; it suggests the Oxbridge establishment. Fitzgerald himself said that by the time he was sixteen he had read Thackeray over and over. To John Peale Bishop he wrote that "Gatsby was shooting at something like *Henry Esmond* while this [*Tender is the Night*] was shooting at something like *Vanity*

Fair. Various critics have found influences of Henry James, Edith Wharton, and Joseph Conrad.

Thus despite the war between the two groups of critics, those of the right were in essential agreement with the radicals that American culture was in a parlous state. From opposite positions both groups lambasted middle-class values. Both groups weighed literature by social and political standards.

On the whole the values preached by the radicals were in accord with contemporary psychological and sociological thought; whereas the New Humanists angrily rejected Freudian and sociological interpretations of human behavior. Certainly the radicals were closer to the mainstream of American life and thought—the democratic, melioristic, humanitarian tradition. They deplored any forces which seemed to be repressive whether in morals, industry, or government. The New Humanists with their extreme emphasis on restraint and the will to refrain might profitably have heeded Oliver Wendell Holmes' remark, "Beware of making your moral staple consist of the negative virtues."

Moreover the New Humanists in their rejection of almost the whole of modern American literature had taken an untenable position. In 1930 Seward Collins stated that Babbitt and More "had more important work to do than to try to stem the advance of the shallow and misguided generation that has dominated American letters for twenty years. That would be equivalent to a teacher's spending all his time on the dunce in his class because he was popular with his fellows." [49]

In a collection of essays in 1930 edited by Norman Foerster, fifteen New Humanists were unanimous in condemning all modern tendencies in science, literature, and society. Only one writer, Harry Hayden Clark, found a modern novel to praise, *The Brimming Cup* by Dorothy Canfield. The title of Clark's essay, "Pandora's Box in American Fiction," [50] indicates his general point of view. Stuart Sherman, who before his death in 1926, had found things to praise in Sinclair Lewis, came in for condemnation. In an essay on "Our Critical Spokesmen" Gorham B. Munson complained of "a fatal lack of authority in Sherman, a certain ultimate slackness of mind and purpose." [51] His writing is too democratic: "it has none of Arnold's aristocratic sweetness."

In a reductio ad absurdum of the humanist position Munson stated: "Objectively considered literature may be found to have been in decline, not just for a century and a half or just six hundred years, but almost from its classical sources and from the Scriptures of ancient lands." [52] Eliot set the date of the decline a little later—after Dante. The Renaissance had been a mistake, the nineteenth century a calamity.

The point of the foregoing discussion is that in the second and third decades of this century, critics too often started with a priori assumptions about human values and about American culture. The iconoclasts rejected that culture as too Puritan; the rightists rejected it as lacking in standards of conduct. It is ironic that the two streams flowed together. The Spoon Rivers, the Winesburgs, the Gopher Prairies which indicted a puritanical society served the rightists as an argument for an authoritarian and aristocratic order.

It is significant that Mencken and Lewis were often coupled as belonging to the same literary movement. Critics tended to speak of them as a team like Webber and Fields. Writing for *The Dial* in 1925 Robert Morss Lovett, after saying that our favorite prophets like Wilson, Harding, and Coolidge were "sayers of smooth things," added:

And yet by some sort of saving grace, in the midst of this complacency appears Mr. Lewis and Mr. Mencken to tear the hoods and sheets off our moral and civic Ku Klux Klan, to show the cringing forms and the false, cowardly, cruel faces beneath the mask—and *Mr. Mencken and Mr. Lewis as critic and novelist are, in this day and generation, the most read and considered interpreters of American life.* [Ital. mine.] [53]

There were similarities, of course: both men exposed some of the shoddier features of American culture, both admired many of the same writers—Drieser, Masters, Cabell, Hergesheimer; both attacked Howells and the New Humanists. But essentially the two men started from different corners of the field and they ended up in separate camps. As has been shown, Mencken shared with More, Babbitt and company a contempt for democracy; whereas Lewis, insofar as he had any ideology, was essentially in the Jeffersonian, Jacksonian tradition—the heir of Howe, Garland, Frederic, and Norris. Thus in his Nobel Prize speech he could praise not only Cabell and Hergesheimer but also Upton Sinclair and John Dos Passos. As Lewis once said, he could understand George F. Babbitt because he had a lot of Babbitt in himself. He could have said the same thing about Dr. Kenicott.

Unlike Mencken and the New Humanists, Lewis understood the basic decency, even the idealism, of the common man beneath his crass exterior. It is no accident that Lewis wrote an anti-facist novel, whereas Mencken wound up in the political bed with More, Babbitt, Pound, and Collins. T. S. Eliot occupied an adjoining room.

The novelists and poets like Masters, Sandburg, Anderson, Dreiser, and Lewis had a visceral understanding of the nature of American life even when they attacked certain features of it; the critics, whether Menckenite or New Humanist, who longed for the aristocratic mansion with the pillared portico never did understand their own culture. As a literary critic Mencken praised more mediocrities than major figures; his championship of Huneker, Dreiser, and Lewis must be balanced by his failure to recognize Joyce, Eliot, Hemingway, Fitzgerald, Wallace Stevens, or Faulkner. As the discoverers of new talent even William Dean Howells had a higher batting average. The New Humanists consistently struck out.

4.

Antidemocratic Vistas

It was not only modern literature which came under attack. A major theme which runs through the writing of intellectuals between 1915 and 1930 is disillusion with American democracy. This is related to but by no means the same thing as the exposures of corruption in business, industry and government. As a rule, the muckrakers and reform candidates for office were not trying to overturn the American system of government but to improve it. On the other hand many intellectuals tended to chase off after Marxist, Anarchist, or Fascist ideas.

The problem at this point is to define the terms *reformer, muckraker, intellectual.* Obviously the same person might, like Upton Sinclair, be all of these. Woodrow Wilson, an intellectual, was briefly a reformer. Theodore Roosevelt, a reformer, was a part-time intellectual. And despite his contemptuous use of the term *muckrake,* T.R. could use the implement himself in attacks on "malefactors of great wealth."

For the purpose of the present discussion, the term

muckraker will be applied chiefly to a journalist exploring the murky depths of American life; *reformer* will be used to describe political activists; *intellectual* will designate the person—whether professor, essayist, novelist, dramatist, or poet—who is more concerned wtih the world of ideas than with that of action. Categories can of course lead to distortion and oversimplification. The reason for using them here is to point out that despite all overlappings and shadowy boundaries there developed in the period under consideration a real cleavage between the intellectual and American society. The intellectual tended to reject most of the values of that society.

On the other hand the muckrakers and reformers as a group were not alienated from the society they hoped to improve. The first group were largely journalists writing for such popular magazines as *Colliers, The American Magazine, World's Work, Everybody's, The Cosmopolitan* and, above all, for *McClure's*. As David Chalmers points out in his study of the muckrakers, "The writers of magazine exposés were basically moderates in most fields. They spoke as representatives of the middle classes of the nation's cities and towns. . . ." They did not preach the doctrine of class warfare. Even the socialism of Upton Sinclair "was not extreme and contained only a limited amount of Marxian paraphernalia." [1]

More than others of these writers Sinclair tended to be the ideologist preaching such panaceas as communal living, vegetarianism, and total abstinence. (He suffered from digestive and marital troubles.) He shared with many intellectuals a yearning for quick, utopian solutions. Thus in 1904 he predicted that six months after the Presidential election of 1908 the American people would have the Socialist program in full operation. In *The Jungle* (1906) he pushed the date ahead to 1912. In *The Industrial Republic* (1907) he saw William Randolph Hearst as the messiah who, pledged to put an end to class government, would be the Democratic candidate.[2] Because of strikes, unemployment and bloodshed, Hearst would defeat Theodore Roosevelt and the "Industrial Republic" would begin.

Sinclair was not alienated from the democratic and Christian ideals of American society. The socialism he preached was to be brought about by means of the ballot. Like a number of his contemporaries, for example, Carl Sandburg, Sinclair considered Christ's teachings a radical force which had been corrupted by wealth and the churches.[3] Sinclair's socialism was basically the humanitarian American variety later preached by Norman Thomas. As late as 1966 Thomas could say, "I've never been alienated, to use the current fashionable term. . . ."[4]

Alienation can of course be a matter of degree. A social critic may reject certain features of a society which he basically respects. On the other hand many of the intellectuals of the period under discussion attacked the fundamental premises of American government.

The will to believe the worst about the American system is reflected in the wide acceptance of Charles Beard's thesis that the Constitution was the result of a conspiracy by the monied interests who imposed the document upon a largely disfranchised public. As has been noted, a study in 1935 showed that 37 out of 45 recent college texts had adopted the Beard thesis. Among those who praised *An Economic Interpretation of the Constitution of the United States* were Walter Lippmann, Albert Jay Nock, Samuel Eliot Morison, John Chamberlain, and Henry Steele Commager.* [5] As will appear, it influenced a

---

* At a later date both Morison and Commager rejected the Beard thesis. Cf. note on Commager, p. 111 below. In *The Oxford History of the American People* (New York, 1965, pp. 306–07) Morison adopts Madison's view.

variety of social critics during the twenties and thirties. As recently as 1950 *An American History* by Merle Curti, Richard H. Shryock, Thomas C. Cochran, and Fred Harvey Harrington largely accepted the Beard doctrine. They state that the delegates were "agreed that in such a central government, control should be lodged with the upper classes." Like Beard the writers stress the point that "the upper classes stood to gain by this strengthening of the central government." They add that "The wealthier groups included many speculators in western lands, which lands would appreciate in value if a national government was strong enough to control the Indians." [6] They go on to point out the advantages to the business classes, and also, like Beard, they imply that the Constitution disadvantaged other classes.

It is ironic that these later historians found that the strong national government thus set up has now become the bulwark of civil rights and the leading instrument in social legislation. At the time Beard wrote, this situation did not obtain. In that era the Senate was, with much justice, considered to represent chiefly the railroads, the big bankers, and the trusts. The Federal courts continued to issue injunctions against strikes; the Supreme Court struck down social legislation such as laws against child labor.

Unwittingly Beard was in accord with a conservative Supreme Court which read back into the original document the views of the National Association of Manufacturers and the American Bankers Association. As Beard stated his thesis:

Suppose . . . that substantially all the merchants, money lenders, security holders, manufacturers, capitalists and financiers and their professional associates are to be found on one side in support of the Constitution and that substantially all or the major portion of the opposition came from the non-slave-holding farmers and debtors—could it not be pretty conclusively demonstrated that our fundamental law was not the product of an abstraction known as "the whole people" but of a group of economic interests which must have expected beneficial results from its adoption.[7]

As Franklin Roosevelt used to say, "That's a very iffy question." Beard admitted that the data was at that time very fragmentary as to the geographic distribution of money, of public securities, of small mortgaged farms, of manufacturing establishments, and about the owners and operators in western lands.

Furthermore Beard's writing is loaded with semantic booby traps. Words like *manufacturers, capitalists,* and *financiers* had meanings in 1913 that were by no means the same as those of 1787. In the earlier period a "manufacturer" was likely to be an artisan running a small operation with the help of his sons and two or three hired hands. He worked at the forge or the lathe or the bench with his own hands to turn out hardware, furniture, wagons or harness. Old engravings and existing buildings testify to the small scale of most eighteenth-century American mills, factories, and iron works. The capitalist in the sense of an owner of large enterprises employing many workingmen was rare. Even Beard admitted that labor had not coalesced as a class. The reason was, of course, that there was often no clear distinction between the artisan, the manufacturer, and the business man. The owner of a mill or a workshop was likely to be all three. Franklin is a case in point. He was printer, bookseller, and a small "capitalist," but he continued to sign himself "Benjamin Franklin, Printer." Paul Revere was a silversmith, a manufacturer, and a contractor in copper sheathing.

Beard's semantic shenanigans are best seen in his selection of categories. Thus in listing the Pennsylvania delegates who favored the Constitution at the convention for ratification he used the term *Securities* to classify the economic interest of such delegates as clergymen, lawyers, a grist-mill owner with 95 acres, a local postmaster, and a surgeon. But in 1787 or even 1887 the lawyer or doctor outside of large cities more often invested his money in a farm than in securities. And of course the clergyman as a rule had no money to invest in either. Just how a postmaster or a grist-mill owner represented the security interests is not clear. But when Beard came to the opponents of the Constitution he did not use this term to apply to the following: a farmer-mill owner, another mill owner, lawyers, and iron masters. On the other hand he listed the iron-master, Coleman, who favored the Constitution, as representing Securities. Thus Beard loaded the dice to show the power of the personality interests.

He used the word *disfranchised* with the same looseness:

> . . . the disfranchisement of the masses through property qualifications and ignorance and apathy contributed largely to the facility with which the personality interest representatives carried the day.[8]

Now the man who does not vote because of ignorance or apathy is not disfranchised in the normal meaning of that term.

Beard himself admitted that "How extensive disfran-

chisement was cannot be determined." [9] On the other hand
Robert E. Brown found that the Records of the Convention "show that probably most free men had the vote in
1787." For instance Benjamin Franklin pointed out that
the common people had the vote and would resist any
effort to deprive them of it.[10] Other delegates argued in
the same way—that the people would not accept a constitution which restricted the vote to freeholders. Furthermore
Beard and his disciples in arguing that the Constitution
was designed to curb highly democratic state governments
never mentioned the fact that a number of states had
property qualifications for public office. For instance, in
Massachusetts and North Carolina there was the requirement of a freehold of a thousand pounds for a governor;
in South Carolina the requirement was a settled plantation
or freehold of ten thousand pounds clear of debt. Representatives in the South Carolina legislature had to own
three thousand, five hundred pounds currency. On the
other hand, after much debate, the makers of the Constitution set no property qualifications for any public office in
the new government.

Beard constantly emphasized his point that "the mer-
cantile, manufacturing, security and personality interests"
dominated the convention and then through undemocratic
processes secured the adoption of the new form of government. He was especially fond of the term *personality*. But
his own figures show that in 1787 money on hand or at
interest represented between 4 and 5 percent of the value
of land and buildings.[11] Similarly Brown discovered that
in state after state the value of reality outweighed the value
of personality by a ratio of about 25 to 1.[12] In his study of
the situation in Massachusetts he discovered ". . . instead
of a colonial society of upper and lower classes, rich and
poor, enfranchised and unenfranchised, I found a pre-

dominantly middle-class society in which most men owned property, most men were farmers and most men could vote." [13]

Beard had much to say about the advantages of a strong central government to the holders of tracts of western lands; he failed to point out that the eastern conservatives who feared the popular domination of newly created states were defeated in their attempt to limit their powers or their representation in Congress. As the more conservative delegates feared, the Constitution as adopted made possible the election of an Andrew Jackson. A majority of the delegates had accepted this possibility. The Constitution as adopted was less a victory for a faction than it was, as Madison stated, an attempt to reconcile the interests of various factions. The founding fathers unlike the doctrinaire intellectuals of a later date, were versed in the British tradition of pragmatic compromise.

On the other hand, Beard's unexpressed basic premise was essentially the Marxist one of class conflict. To support it he had to exaggerate class differences and interests. Thus he inflated the holders of securities into a large and powerful class. Yet he admitted that evidence was lacking to show the geographic distribution and ownership of public securities. Beard's clearly implied assumption is that if the Constitution benefited business and industry, it therefore injured the farmer and the artisan. As evidence he noted that when the document was ratified "the several local manufacturing concerns were extensively represented by floats and banners, which shows that they were not unaware of the gain that had been made *in their favor* [Ital. mine] by the establishment of the new system." [14] As has been noted, the term *manufacturing concerns* is highly misleading in the context of 1787. Furthermore other groups also celebrated. John Quincy Adams, who did not favor the

Constitution, noted sourly that in Newburyport "the satisfaction was almost universal;" [15] the bells were rung and
"the mob buzzed." In New York and Philadelphia all
classes joined in the celebration.*

The fact that a book so obviously slanted and based
on admittedly sketchy evidence could be accepted as gospel
can only be explained by the intellectual community's
readiness to accept any derogatory view of the American
scene. This enthusiastic acceptance of *An Economic Interpretation of the Constitution* parallels the enthusiastic
acceptance of Brooks' early views of the American literary
past and of the Masters-Anderson-Lewis picture of the
small town.

An example of this uncritical acceptance of the Beard
thesis is found in V. L. Parrington's *Main Currents in*

* On July 4, 1788, Philadelphia had a parade to celebrate the adoption
of the Constitution. The marchers included military companies and
representatives of the trades and professions. The trades represented
included architects and house carpenters, saw makers and file cutters,
farmers, boat builders, rope makers and ship chandlers, merchants and
traders, cordwainers, cabinet and chair makers, brick makers, house, ship
and sign painters, porters, clock and watch makers, fringe and ribband
weavers, tailors, instrument makers, windsor-chair and spinning-wheel
makers, bricklayers, carvers and gilders, blacksmiths, coach makers, potters,
hatters, wheelwrights, tin-plate workers, skinners, breeches makers and
glovers, tallow chandlers, victuallers, printers, bookbinders and stationers,
saddlers, stonecutters, bread and biscuit makers, gunsmiths, coppersmiths,
goldsmiths, silversmiths and jewellers, distillers, tobacconists, brass founders, stocking manufacturers, tanners, upholsterers, barber surgeons, engrav-
ers, brush makers, plasterers and stay makers.

Each group had its own banner, and a number had elaborate floats
such as that of the printers who had one with a press in operation striking
off copies of a poem written for the occasion by Francis Hopkinson. The
200 blacksmiths had a complete blacksmith shop in operation on a ten by
fifteen foot platform drawn by nine horses. The tailors had 250 men in
the procession, the hatters 126, the coach makers over 160, the bread and
biscuit makers 150. Francis Hopkinson, *The Miscellaneous Essays and
Writings of*, Philadelphia, 1792, II, 349–401.

American Thought (1927). For him the Constitution was "achieved by a skillful minority in the face of a hostile majority. . . . The strategic position of the large property interests in the year 1787 was favorable to a bold stroke." [15a] But eighty pages later Parrington wrote:

> The America of Jefferson's day was a simple domestic economy. More than ninety per cent were plain country folk, farmers and villagers, largely freeholders, managing their local affairs in the traditional way. There were no great extremes of poverty and wealth, no closely organized class groups.[16]

One may be permitted to ask what had become of "the large property interests," the class struggle, the defeat of local self-government which Parrington had talked about in his chapter "Agrarianism and Capitalism."

Beard's contention that economic interests played a part in the making of the Constitution is of course valid. Madison dealt with this in his famous *Federalist Paper* No. 10. But Beard distorted Madison's view: he argued that Madison was interested in furthering class interests. The fact is that Madison was saying that the Constitution made it more difficult for a faction to control government. He pointed out that a class or faction could more easily control a state than a strong national government—a view which events in the coal-and-iron era of Pennsylvania or in twentieth-century Mississippi and Alabama have clearly demonstrated.*

The States Rights enthusiasts who opposed the Constitution or who later set up the Confederacy or who today attack the Federal Government are almost always part of a

* "Enlarge the sphere and balance the interests: has not American history proved Madison's wisdom?" Morison, *Oxford History,* p. 307.

class or faction which seeks special privileges which can be gained more easily through state legislatures.

Neither Beard nor his followers seem to have asked the basic question of whether a national government which had no power to collect taxes, defend the country, pay the public debt, or enforce laws could have survived. Under the Articles of Confederation, defined by the states in Article III as a "firm league of friendship with each other," nine states retained their own navies; Pennsylvania currency could circulate only within the state; states enforced tariff barriers against each other; New Jersey had its own customs service; Virginia provided that ships, including those from other states, which failed to pay duty could be seized.

If the Beard thesis, which he advanced as a hypothesis, had been accepted as a corrective to the demigod myth of the founding fathers, it would have served a useful purpose. But when it was accepted by the intellectuals as an article of faith, it gave aid and comfort to the extremists of the left and right. The Marxists found support for their class war theory of history; the reactionaries saw it as proof that the founding fathers, especially Hamilton, had never really believed in democracy in the first place. It is perhaps not too much to say that *An Economic Interpretation of the Constitution of the United States* was the most destructive document of its era.*

---

* By 1966 Commager had evidently come to reject the Beard thesis:

Some students, treating the Convention as an economic rather than political body, have declared that its chief conclusions favored the property-owning, trading, and creditor "class." But once more we must remember that America in 1787 was a land where nearly all—farmers, planters, shopkeepers, professional men—were well off and class lines few and faint. And security and stability profited everybody, for everybody was interested in stable money, a flourishing trade, the protection of western lands, the firm administration of justice, the efficient admin-

Granville Hicks in explaining the reasons for the 1920s revolt of young intellectuals against the *status quo,* a revolt that eventually carried Hicks and numerous others into the Communist camp, wrote that they were impressed by Veblen and Beard and used *Theory of the Leisure Class* and *An Economic Interpretation of the Constitution* as ammunition against the Philistines.[17] In *Our America* (1919), written, as has been noted, to explain America to the French, Waldo Frank stated that the Constitution secured "the commercial oligarchy which persists to this day." [18] In *Rediscovery of America* (1929) he called the Constitution "an antiquated makeshift constructed by spiritually callous men." [19] One heritage of all this is that a university newspaper run by the "new left" was in 1969 using the Beard thesis to argue for destroying the existing system.

Joining in this mania for idol-breaking, William Carlos Williams argued that Washington and Hamilton had built walls against liberty; whereas Aaron Burr was a defender of liberty.

Early in the 1930s Glenway Wescott entitled a chapter, "Democracy is a Failure." [20] In it, after stating that Jefferson wrote the Constitution, he demanded a new one which

---

istration of everyday affairs of government. And as for the Constitution as a "class" document, it is relevant to observe that under its provisions there were no property or religious qualifications for voting or for any Federal office. Allan Nevins and Henry Steele Commager, *A Short History of the United States,* N. Y., 1966, p. 125.

Speaking of Beard's contention in 1935 for the moral neutrality of the book, Richard Hofstadter writes:

Beard . . . must have been aware that if you picture a set of men as framing a new government in secret by an illegal process and as reaping personal gains from its acceptance, you do not need to pour on the vinegar of indignant rhetoric to achieve a certain acid flavor. *The Progressive Historians,* N. Y., 1968, p. 219.

would set up categories for voting such as laborer, scientist, scholar, etc. One could take an examination to establish his category. Wescott desired to make it unconstitutional for men of state to do secret business of any kind. Diplomatic correspondence, military instructions, even dictaphonic reports of official councils should be printed immediately at government expense.[21]

There is small evidence that the iconoclasts who swallowed Beard whole had much knowledge of American history. They seem not to have read *The Federalist* or in some cases even the Constitution. Nor is there evidence that they had studied the political systems of other countries. Compared to such a thoughtful and judicious discussion of American government as Whitman's *Democratic Vistas,* much of the writing by literary people during the second renaissance bears a striking resemblance to a college bull session.

For instance Margaret Anderson in her avant-garde *Little Review* managed the improbable feat of propagandizing simultaneously for the doctrines of Nietzsche and those of the anarchist, Emma Goldman. In an essay "The Challenge of Emma Goldman" Miss Anderson stated:

> What is she fighting for? For the same things, concertedly, that Nietzsche and Max Sterner fought for abstractly. . . .[22]

Never one to accept compromise or adopt a judicial point of view (her autobiography is called *My Thirty Years War*) Miss Anderson argued:

> Radical changes in society, releasement from present injustices and miseries, can come about not through reform but through *change,* not through a patching

up of the old order, but through a tearing down and rebuilding. This process involves the repudiation of such "spooks" as Christianity, conventional morality and other "myths" that stand as obstacles to progress, freedom, health, truth, and beauty: One thus achieves that position beyond good and evil for which Nietzsche pleaded.[23]

In *The Little Review,* one of several essays on Nietzsche by George Burman Foster is followed without comment by the quote:

Ye say that a good cause will even sanctify war! I tell you, it is the good war that sanctifies every cause! [24]

Margaret Anderson's idea of a good war was reflected in her essay "Art and Anarchism": [25]

Why are you so crazy about the government?

Why do you want to govern anything or anybody?— even your own temper? Nietzsche said not to preserve yourself but to discharge yourself. Why not use your temper as well as your nice moods? . . .

Why do you want to govern human nature? Because you want people to be good instead of bad? But how can you tell when they're good or bad?

You have seen that the blind, stupid thing we call government cannot give you a happy childhood. It cannot educate you or make you an interesting person. It cannot give you work, art, love, or life.

This bull-session spirit also characterized *The Masses,* which called itself "a magazine with a sense of humor, and no respect for the respectable; frank, arrogant, impertinent, searching for the true causes." Alfred Kazin described it as having been "run like a circus wagon." [26] Preaching the class struggle it nevertheless printed art-for-art's sake poetry and even carried jokes about itself and its causes. Edited by Max Eastman and Floyd Dell it had as contributors people as diverse as Gelett Burgess, Amy Lowell, and Genevieve Taggard. Its socialism was not a party-line ideology but was tinged with anarchist and syndicalist doctrines.

Before World War I the left-wing writers shared many of the views of the Progressives, but they tended to reject the gradualist approach of the latter. Furthermore a number of intellectuals who advocated moderate methods were nevertheless sympathetic with advocates of extremist views. Thus Mable Dodge in her salon on Washington Square had as guests the anarchist, Emma Goldman; the I. W. W. leader, Bill Haywood; the Socialists, Floyd Dell and Max Eastman; the young radicals John Reed and Walter Lippmann.[27] They discussed socialism, anarchism, Freud, and Jung. Here Lincoln Steffens heard talk "of the plotted blowing-up by the structural iron workers of the steel work of buildings and bridges as a part of the very real war of labor in the U. S. and other steel companies, and [he] felt something of the passion which prompted a responsible labor organization to turn to the systematic use of dynamite. . . ." [28]

In 1924 Floyd Dell looking back to the pre-war period wrote:

> Up to 1914, I was, like the rest of the civilized world, a believer in the gospel of force. Like the Kaiser and Sir Edward Grey, and Colonel Roosevelt and the McNamara boys, I believed that a judicious use of high explosives would bring to pass a kingdom of heaven on earth.[29]

One of the heroes of Mabel Dodge's salon was Big Bill Haywood, whose I. W. W. condoned violence in labor disputes. When in 1912 the Socialist Party attempted to woo the A. F. of L. by adopting a resolution to expel all members who advocated the use of violence, Haywood pulled the I. W. W. out of the party.[30] In *The Masses* Max Eastman wrote fire-breathing editorials demanding that labor unite to seize industrial sovereignty.[31]

However it was Floyd Dell who came to recognize the doctrinaire quality of the radicalism of the time. In 1926 he wrote that the intellectuals

> . . . saw the working class as the protagonists of the future and cast in our lot emotionally with its hope [but] the trade unions had their own vision of their goal, and despite their temporary fighting moods, it was a sedate and respectable vision. They were shocked at ours. They did not want to overthrow capitalism; they wanted lace curtains and a piano in their homes.[32]

Writing in *The Masses* in 1916 Helen Marot bemoaned the fact that "the railroad trainmen did not do any of the things that the revolutionists would like them to do. They did not strike." [33]

However, some of the left-wing intellectuals began to have their doubts about a benevolent national ownership of industry. State Capitalism began to seem the final triumph of the enemy. Workmen could strike against private industry but not against the state. This explains some intellectuals' flirtation with the anarchists. As Dell said, "Perhaps—we young parliamentarian Socialists began to think—we had been fighting doggedly on the wrong side. If it was the State which was the greatest obstacle to the achievement of human happiness, what were we doing with our parlimentarianism but fostering it." [34] But the anarchists he knew were gentle people; there was not a dynamiter in the lot. In any case the State was too strong to overthrow. Therefore the anarchists turned their attention to freedom in relations between men and women. They spoke reverently of John and Mary who had been defying convention by living together for nearly sixty years.[35]

The intellectuals also flirted with the syndicalist doctrine that the workmen should control the factories—a doctrine embedded in I. W. W. ideology. All of these ideologies—Marxist, anarchist, and syndicalist—shared a misunderstanding of the complexities of industrial and economic organization.* They largely overlooked the role of leadership and management: economic forces would take care of all this. The workers, the proletariat would somehow, without training and experience, be able to control processes that often baffle the experts. According to Marx, once the dictatorship of the proletariat was established, the state would wither away. Had the theorists carried their doctrines to a logical conclusion they would have recognized that the complexities and close interrelationships of technology, production and distribution would lead inevitably to centralized control either by combinations of bankers and industrialists or by a powerful central government.

The leftists made two other basic mistakes: they underestimated the social and economic gains of the American people, and under the influence of Marx, they developed an oversimplified view of the class structure.

Before Wilson's second term as President, the Progressives had achieved more of their program for social

* It is worth noting that J. J. Servan-Schreiber in *The American Challenge* (1968) argues that the skills of American management are the chief reason for American economic domination.

control of business and industry than the radicals were willing to admit. Despite political corruption and special privilege there was during the Progressive era a considerable amount of social legislation: the pure food laws; some trust busting; greater regulation of public utilities; state-by-state development of laws limiting child labor and the work hours for women; safety standards for mines and factories; the banning of the old-law tenements in New York; the creation in 1913 of The Federal Reserve System, despite the prediction of bankers that it would produce a bank panic. What is often overlooked is that there was also an ever increasing support of public education all the way to the university level. Between 1900 and 1930 the proportion of high school graduates rose from about ten percent to fifty percent of that age group.

Social pressures had generated the development of large public universities; and the muckrakers' exposure of business corruption had tenderized the consciences of some of the malefactors of great wealth to cause them to try to improve their images by huge gifts to colleges and universities. These institutions quickly began to serve a rapidly increasing number of students. In 1900 the percentage of 18 to 21 year olds in college was 4.01; by 1920 it had more than doubled to 8.14; in 1930 it had increased to 12.37. This is only one indication of the spreading economic well being of vast numbers of Americans.

In 1906 Woodrow Wilson had stated that "nothing has spread socialistic feeling in this country more than the use of the automobile." [36] The reverse was of course true. As early as 1901 the very practical curved-dash Oldsmobile was being mass produced at $650. Some of them are still running. The famous Model T Ford appeared on the scene late in 1908 at $850. In 1925 the

Ford roadster listed at $260. By 1926 there was one auto-
mobile for every five persons in the United States. It was
becoming increasingly difficult to persuade Americans that
capitalism was the enemy of the people.

Of course Utopia had not arrived. Steel workers still
had a twelve-hour day until Harding pressured the industry
to introduce the eight-hour day in 1923; [37] knitting mill
operators and garment workers were grossly underpaid;
the courts and the police joined hands to break strikes.
Because of the fact that a high proportion of workers in
these industries were foreign born or second generation
Americans, they were suspect in the eyes of both the middle
class and the Populists. The latter group, which had
captured the Democratic party in 1896 to nominate Bryan,
was largely rural and small-town. It was puritanical,
Protestant, and xenophobic. In contrast, the urban and
industrial proletariat was not only "foreign," it was pre-
dominately Catholic and Jewish. One group supported
Prohibition; the other detested it.

The left-wing intellectuals like Max Eastman and
Floyd Dell who made *The Masses* such a lively journal,
tended to apply Marxist theory to the American political
and economic scene. Thus they oversimplified the class
struggle: proletariat versus capitalists. The real situation
was more complex because of unique American conditions.
In the older societies of Europe class lines were more
sharply drawn: workers versus capitalists and land holders.
In the United States class divisions were complex and
shifting. Social mobility was not only possible but frequent.
Within the ranks of labor there was a division between
the older craft unions holding essentially middle-class
views as contrasted with the I. W. W. committed to the
idea of revolutionary change. Old stock Americans of
the working class tended to consider themselves socially

superior to more recent arrivals. Negroes were of course relegated to a special caste and were excluded by the trade unions. In the recognition of the great variety of economic interests in the United States it was Madison rather than the Marxists who drew the more accurate picture.

On the basis of a report by Steffens, Max Eastman in *The Masses* (August 1917) wrote, "the facts fall out exactly as they were predicted by Marx and Engels and the philosophers of Syndicalism." [38] (He of course overlooked the fact that Marx had predicted that the proletarian revolution would first occur in highly industrialized countries and that it was not the proletariat but a small disciplined minority which had taken over the Russian government.) Eastman went on, "The control of the factories by the workingmen's unions is practically universal. . . . The Council of Workingmen's and Soldiers' Deputies is in absolute control. . . ." Eastman made fun of a *New York Times* dispatch describing the chaos in Russian factories. "Now I know that the whole dream [of control by the workers] has come true . . . I call Lincoln Steffens the friend of Revolutions. . . . And when Lincoln Steffens, after five weeks in Petrograd, tells me that he will never be sad again—I know that the essence of liberty is there."

In *Writers on the Left* Daniel Aaron has extensively documented the tendency of leftists who visited Russia during the twenties to find what they were looking for. As Aaron puts it:

> To the small body of convinced Communists in the United States, the Soviet republic by 1926 was no longer an experiment, but an unqualified success in social planning, "as fresh, as new and beautiful," wrote the enraptured Mike Gold, "as first love."

. . . He had not expected Utopia, but he found he could relax in a place "so primitive, so easy going, so good natured." [39]

This kind of misty-eyed sentimentality is easier to forgive than was the willingness of American left-wing intellectuals to jettison the genuine values of their own culture. Granted that there were many flaws in that culture, it was nevertheless one which had conquered or mitigated many ancient tyrannies. Based on the Judeo-Christian tradition of justice and mercy, on the British ideal of individual freedom from arbitrary government, and on the American emphasis on the right of people to choose their own beliefs, this society was in theory, if not always in practice, committed to humane values—what the left wing increasingly called bourgeois values. Under Max Eastman *The Liberator* endorsed the Third International and likened Marxism and Leninism to the discoveries of Copernicus, Kepler and Newton. He dismissed phrases like "political democracy," "liberty," "suffrage," "responsible government," "free speech," "the right of assembly," "the people," as liberal catchwords or "plausible ideologies" or "moralistic disguises" of a ruinous capitalism.[40] Lincoln Steffens accepted Lenin's statement that dictatorship did not carry with it "much risk of tyranny": terror was only an unavoidable phase. Steffens asked if it mattered whether he or Emma Goldman got liberty. "An important thing is that Bolshevik Russia shall go through its tyranny patiently and arrive at liberty for the whole Russian people and perhaps for the world." [41]

This is of course the old argument that the end justifies the means. But as Aldous Huxley once pointed out, means become ends. The suppression of dissent for the accomplishment of an immediate end can eventually become the suppression of dissent as an ideology. The American experience after World War I is a case in point. The prosecutions and jailings of pacifists and opponents of the draft was followed in peace time by the greatest assault on civil liberties in our history.

Even intellectual liberals became infected with the notion that a temporary suppression of liberty would lead to a better world. It is significant that the Palmer raids and deportations grew out of the crusade to make the world safe for democracy. In 1927 *The New Republic* undertook an apologia for the Fascism of Mussolini.[42] It printed an article by Horace M. Kallen, who argued that "Mussolini is carrying on the work which the heroes of the Risorgimento began." In the same issue the editors said that there was much to be said in favor of Kallen's warning to liberals who deplored Mussolini:

> A dictatorship by a faction under the leadership of one man will doubtless look to many of our readers like anything but an experiment in self-government, but sceptics should remember that the effort of a community to govern itself may assume many forms.[43]

Critics of fascism were cautioned against "outlawing a political experiment which arouses in a whole nation an increased moral energy and dignifies its activities by subordinating them to a deeply felt common purpose." [44]

This was essentially the same argument used by the left-wing defenders of Bolshevik despotism. It grows out of the intellectual's tendency to demand drastic solutions to social and political problems.*

---

* It is worth noting that left-wing intellectuals like Herbert Marcuse and the Students for a Democratic Society are today preaching similar doctrines.

The scope of this chapter does not permit a detailed analysis of the intellectual left before 1930—an analysis to which Aaron devotes over two-hundred pages. Nor does it take into account the effects of the great depression after that date. Obviously the apparent collapse of the capitalistic system and the rise of Nazism justified a searching examination of the values of the old order. Events in Germany clearly suggested that Nazism was an end-product of capitalism. Too many British and American conservatives hailed Hitler as the antidote to Russian Communism. The expressed ideals of Communism were certainly preferable to those of Hitler.

The failure of so many intellectuals to recognize the similarities of the two systems had its roots in the self-deceptions of the leftist intellectuals of the twenties. The shelf of *mea culpa* books written by the penitents has made the record boringly familiar. Granville Hicks could be speaking for most of his fellow travelers when he described his "two major blind spots:"

> (1) I refused to see that the Communist party of the United States was completely subservient to the Soviet Union; (2) I would not admit to myself that the Soviet Union was basically and incurably a totalitarian dictatorship.[45]

Hicks put the case against himself bluntly, *"Mistakes in judgment are exactly the kind of mistakes for which an intellectual cannot be forgiven."* [Ital. mine] [46]

Hicks and the others who later acknowledged that they were fantastically mistaken fail to go back to the root causes of that kind of mistake. These writers cite the admitted evils they were trying to combat: economic injustice, Philistinism, greed, intolerance, repressive morality, political corruption—all the unlovely features of

American life, especially in the period from Wilson's re-election to the inauguration of Franklin Roosevelt. However, many liberal politicians were trying to combat these same evils, men like the two Robert LaFollettes, Gifford Pinchot, Alfred E. Smith, George W. Norris, Fiorello LaGuardia. As governors, senators, congressmen, and mayors they successfully promoted progressive measures even in the depths of the Harding-Coolidge era. Under Franklin Roosevelt the Populist, Progressive, and Labor movements of the preceding forty or fifty years showed their continuing vitality.

It must be granted, of course, that between 1918 and 1932 the business community and the government which it so largely controlled did much to prove the class-war doctrines of the radical left. Calvin Coolidge's statement that "the business of America is business" represented the ruling philosophy. Conservative boards of trustees dismissed college professors whose economic or political views clashed with those of the business community. There had been dismissals even before the 1920s, notably that of Professor Edward A. Ross from Stanford because of his advocacy of free silver, municipal ownership of utilities and his opposition to the importation of cheap labor from Japan.

No faculty firing up to that time had so dramatized the issue of wealth versus academic freedom. The American Economic Association appointed a distinguished committee to investigate the case. The academic community began to organize in its own defense against an enemy that seemed all too often to be the business community. In 1915 the American Association of University Professors was organized chiefly to defend academic freedom.

At Columbia Nicholas Murray Butler either fired or caused the resignation of such prominent men as the composer Edward MacDowell; the poet and professor of

English, George Edward Woodberry; the editor and critic, Harry Thurston Peck, founder of *The Bookman;* and Joel E. S. Spingarn, the literary critic. During the war Butler dismissed the distinguished psychologist J. McKeen Cattell for asking members of Congress to support a bill against sending draftees to Europe against their will. Charles A. Beard resigned in sympathy with a letter to *The New York Times* stating:

> . . . I have been driven to the conclusion that the university is really under the control of a small and active group of trustees who have no standing in the world of education, who are reactionary and visionless in politics, narrow and medieval in religion.[47]

During the 1920s thousands of faculty members could have echoed this statement. In 1921 Vice-President Coolidge wrote for the *Delineator* a series of articles entitled "Enemies of the Republic!" The first of these was subtitled: "Are the Reds Stalking our College Women?" Under a subheading, "Hotbed of Bolshevism" he quoted with horrified italics a line from a speech before a Socialist Club at Radcliffe: *"Every society must have a state, and we must not stop with the United States of America, but must go on and achieve the United States of the World."* He further cited as dangerous the statement in the *News* that, *"A genuine democratization of industry must be brought about."* Coolidge reported that at Wellesley there was a professor who was "said to have voted for Debs."

In his muckraking study of the colleges, *The Goose Step* (1923), Upton Sinclair documented the widespread suppression of academic freedom in America. Professors testified to a pervasive atmosphere of fear which led them to be careful of what they said. At a midwestern university a local business group sent stenographers to follow faculty members about town, taking down their speeches. A California group employed well-to-do students to spy on students and faculty suspected of harboring radical views. A leading publisher of college textbooks submitted them for approval by representatives of privately owned public utilities. It is small wonder that a great many faculty members, especially those in the social sciences, developed a sense of alienation. By the time of Franklin Roosevelt's so-called brain trust, newspaper cartoonists frequently represented the man in academic cap and gown as a wild-eyed radical. It is hardly an exaggeration to say that the business community which dominated the United States in the period under discussion pushed faculty members to the left—particularly those faculty members most concerned with political, social, and economic matters.

The great watershed of the 1920s was of course the Sacco-Vanzetti case. The details of the case are beyond the scope of this chapter, but it soon boiled down to a contest between those who wanted to stamp out dissent and those who defended the constitutional guarantees of free speech and fair trial. The intellectuals began to discover that those in power were not to be moved by thoughtful articles in even the most respectable periodicals, like *The Atlantic*. The Episcopal Bishop of Massachusetts, William Lawrence, spoke for his class as he had in 1901 when he called strikes a form of brigandage, and said that "it is only to the man of morality that wealth comes." He congratulated Governor Fuller and expressed "admiration for the way in which you have done your duty in the Sacco-Vanzetti case."

Originally the cause of Sacco and Vanzetti had been championed by the left-wing press but it came to arouse much of the intellectual community. Among the writers arrested for parading in front of the State House were John Dos Passos, Dorothy Parker, and Edna St. Vincent Millay. Sixty-seven-year old Ellen Hayes, head of the English Department at Wellesley, stated "I feel I must voice a protest." She too was arrested for picketing the State House. In a final appeal a telegram was sent to President Coolidge, signed by David Starr Jordan, Oswald Garrison Villard, Glenn Frank, Alexander Meikeljohn, Benjamin B. Lindsey, Arthur Garfield Hayes, Ida Tarbell, Rockwell Kent, Carl Van Doren, John F. Hylan, Floyd Dell and Otto Soglow. Three of these were, or had been college presidents; one was a Columbia professor. Their alliance with writers, artists, liberal lawyers, and a New York mayor was prophetic of the social alignment of the next decade. The Sacco-Vanzetti case pushed many liberals into the camp of the radicals. As Edmund Wilson said twenty years later, the execution of these men "made the liberals lose their bearings."

What the liberals often failed to realize was that the Marxists and Communists were as cynical in their defense of constitutional rights as was the business community. Sacco and Vanzetti and the Scottsboro boys were useful as martyrs; in fact the Communist intervention in the Scottsboro case probably damaged the cause. As has been noted, the Communists defended the suppression of civil liberties in Russia and, like Eastman, decried as catch words of bourgeois capitalism such terms as, political democracy, liberty, suffrage, free speech, and the right of assembly.

Unlike the intellectuals of the radical left who tended to affiliate with organized groups such as the I. W. W. or the Socialist Party, those of the radical right usually confined their activities to fulminating in print. The mass movement of leftists into the Communist party during the 1930s has been extensively documented by a variety

of penitents, but because of the much less extensive literature of recantation on the part of the rightists, the extent of their acceptance of antidemocratic doctrines has
received less attention. Also the right wingers, with the
exception of Pound, were rarely made to suffer for their
convictions. Groups such as The American Legion, the
House Un-American Activities Committee, and boards of
trustees tended to let them alone.

But just as the logic of the left before 1930 carried
so many of its subscribers into the Communist camp after
that date, so the doctrines of the right made them hospi-
table to fascist doctrines.

As might be expected, the writers who longed for a
literature of the pillared portico carried the same view
into political theory. Unlike the leftists with their utopian
prophecies the right-wing intellectuals tended to be bitter
and pessimistic. Even the surface joviality of Mencken
could not disguise an essential malevolence. For him the
science of politics was merely "a combat between jackals
and jackasses. It is the master transaction of democratic
states." [48] Almost the whole of *Notes on Democracy* (1926)
is a series of assertions of a like nature. Thus

> The whole life of the inferior man, including his
> so-called thinking, is purely a biochemical process, and
> exactly comparable to what goes on in a barrel of
> cider.[49]

It might be noted that whatever went on in Mencken's
mind, the results were as predictable as that cider would
turn into vinegar.

Such evidence as he cited was chiefly contemporary:
Comstockery, Prohibition, the Tennessee law against teaching the theory of evolution. Mencken showed no interest

in the examples of progressive or enlightened legislation of the preceding twenty years, such things as pure food laws, workmen's compensation, the creation of the Federal Reserve, the prohibition against discriminatory freight rates, the beginnings of the conservation of natural resources. If a few states prohibited the teaching of evolution, a greater number prohibited child labor, limited the working hours of women, and set up safety standards for mines and factories.

In fact for all his parade of being a knowledgeable fellow Mencken often revealed a very superficial learning. Just as he showed a very sketchy acquaintance with American literature, he accepted the Beard clichés about our history. Stating that the Revolution was imposed upon the common people by their betters he went on: "Universal manhood suffrage, the corner-stone of modern free states, was only dreamed of until 1867, and economic freedom was little more than a name until years later." [50] Like so many other writers of the time, Mencken never took the trouble to examine the evidence—evidence which, as Brown discovered, showed that in 1787 most men owned property and most free men could vote. In fact, contemporary documents like Franklin's *Information for Those Who Would Remove to America* (1782) and Crèvecoeur's *Letters from an American Farmer* (1782) testify to the widespread ownership of property and the equalitarian nature of eighteenth-century American society. Both Franklin and Crèvecoeur went into some detail to show the easy transition of laborer into freeholder.

Much of what Mencken had to say about democracy was on the intellectual level of the pronouncements of the John Birch Society. He described the House of Representatives as "comparable to a gang of bootleggers" [51] in intelligence, information, and integrity. Our laws were "invented in the main by frauds and fanatics, and put on the statute books by poltroons and scoundrels." [52] According to Mencken democracy was "in greater peril of the free spirit than any sort of despotism ever heard of. . . . It could not endure dissent of the kind permitted by Frederick the Great." [53]

The difference between Mencken's era and that of the John Birch Society is that the intellectuals of the 1920s mistook Mencken for a serious thinker. For instance, *The Nation* said of *Notes on Democracy*, "It is Mr. Mencken at his very fine best." [54] In *The Saturday Review of Literature* Walter Lippmann commented that some of Mencken's ideas were confused, but went on to say, "What Mr. Mencken has created is a personal force in American life which has an extraordinary cleansing and vitalizing effect." [55]

Mencken tended to regard himself as a disciple of Friedrich Nietzsche's. In 1921, *Vanity Fair* elected Mencken to its "Hall of Fame," "Because he wrote one of the first and best books on Nietzsche" [56] and again in 1924 "Because he has contributed more to the popular understanding of Nietzsche than any other American." Ernest Boyd argued that Mencken created Nietzsche in his own image. In any case Mencken represented Nietzsche as the foe of Christianity, democracy, socialism, and humanitarianism. He quoted Nietzsche as saying that the ideal laboring class is "a class content to obey without question." It is not surprising therefore that in the 1930s Mencken condoned the policies of Hitler.

The similarity of Mencken's views and those of the New Humanists has already been noted. Thus Paul Elmer More stated that "the rights of property are more important than the right to life." [57] Irving Babbitt's dislike of universal suffrage has already been cited. He also held that

"Every form of social justice, indeed tends toward confis-
cation." [58] In 1924 he wrote: "Circumstances may arise
when we may esteem ourselves fortunate if we get the
American equivalent of a Mussolini; he may save us from
the American equivalent of a Lenin." [59]

Probably the most notorious apologist for Italian
Fascism was Ezra Pound. Starting out as a convert to
the doctrine of Social Credit propounded by the Scot's
engineer, C. H. Douglas, Pound came to believe that a
small group, chiefly Jewish bankers like the Rothschilds,
the de Mandels, the Comite de Forges had gained control
of "financial credit" at the expense of "real credit" which
was the rightful property of the people who produced it.

In *Hugh Selwyn Mauberly* Pound sneered at a free
press and democratic institutions:

> You have the press for wafer
> Franchise for circumcision.

As early as 1926 he wrote to Harriet Monroe:

> I personally think extremely well of Mussolini. If
> one compares him to American presidents (the last
> three) or British premiers, etc., in fact one can NOT
> without insulting him. [60]

By 1942 he was broadcasting to Americans:

> Had you had the sense to eliminate Roosevelt and his
> Jews and the Jews and their Roosevelt at the last elec-
> tion, you would not now be at war. [61]

And in May of that year:

The kike, and the unmitigated evil that has been centered in London since the British government set on the Red Indians to murder the American frontier settlers, has herded the Slavs, the Mongols, the Tartar openly against Germany and Poland and Finland, and secretly against all that is decent in America. . . .[62]

It is significant that T. S. Eliot was both a disciple of Irving Babbitt's and an admirer of Pound. Even in his early poems Eliot showed a clear anti-Semitic bias. In *Burbank with a Baedeker: Bleistein with a Cigar,* Bleistein is described as "Chicago Semite Viennese," and is represented as having "a lustreless protrusive eye [which] stares from the protozoic slime." The next stanza states:

. . . On the Rialto once
The rats are underneath the piles.
The Jew is underneath the lot.
Money in furs.

And in *Sweeney among the Nightingales* one of the whores is carefully identified as "Rachel *nee* Rabinovitch."

By 1933 Eliot was telling an audience at the *University of Virginia* that in a Christian society "reasons of race and religion combine to make any large number of free-thinking Jews undesirable." He saw chances for a native culture to be better in the South than in New England because "You are farther away from New York; you have been less industrialized and *less invaded by foreign races.* . . ." [Ital. mine]. For Eliot a true culture or tradition "involves all those habitual actions, habits and customs . . . which represent the blood kinship of the same people living in the same place." [63]

Remarks such as these take on added significance because of the context of the time. Eliot gave his talk the same year in which Hitler became chancellor of Germany and it was published as *Under Strange Gods* in 1934 at a time when anti-Semitism was being enacted into German law. It is true that Eliot later came to regard "the ethically inert and negative society of the democracies as better at least than positive evil." [64] That is a little like the boy who plays with matches but is shocked by a burning house.

It is true that as early as 1929 Eliot, in *The Criterion* had pointed out the similarities between fascism and communism, but added, "I confess to a preference for fascism in practice, which I dare say most of my readers share; and I will not admit that this preference is itself wholly irrational. I believe that the fascist form of unreason is less remote from my own than is that of the communists." [65]

What Eliot really preferred was of course royalism, by which he seems to have meant something more autocratic than the British constitutional monarchy. Along with Babbitt and Mencken he was contemptuous of the common man whom he represented in several poems as Sweeney. For Eliot "The governing elite of a nation as a whole, would consist of those whose responsibility was inherited with their position and affluence." [66] "At moments when the public interest is aroused," wrote Eliot, "the public is never well informed enough to have the right to an opinion." Commenting on this, Charles Norman pointed out that the choices made by such intellectuals as Pound and Eliot in the decades which shattered the western world did not demonstrate their superior right to opinion.[67]

Walter Lippmann, who greed with Eliot that it was difficult if not impossible "for the mass of voters to form significant public opinions," recognized that this was not because of "a congenital difference between the masterful few and the ignorant many;" it was that "only the insider can make decisions, not because he is inherently a better man but because he is so placed that he can understand and can act." This business of being an outsider applied not only to the common man; it was the reason "why excellent automobile manufacturers, literary critics, and scientists often talk such nonsense about politics." [68]

By contrast the common man in a modern complex society could often handle himself very well. Lippmann cited the remarks of Herbert Hoover, who during a Mississippi flood set up ninety-one local committees in as many communities:

> . . . A couple of thousand refugees are coming. They've got to have accommodations. Huts, Water Mains, Sewers, Streets, Dining halls, Meals, Doctors, Everything. . . . So you go away and they go ahead and just simply do it. Of those ninety-one committees there was just one that fell down.[69]

Hoover was quoted by his campaign biographer as adding, "No other Main Street in the world could have done what the American Main Street did in the Mississippi flood. . . . The safety of the United States is in its multitudinous mass leadership." [70]

However it is rare in the period under discussion to find intellectuals like Lippmann with kind words for American democracy. The left-wing writers were more or less spokesmen for a dictatorship of the proletariat, the right wingers for an oligarchy of race and class. Just as

Dell, Eastman, and Steffens tried to identify with the horny-handed and horny-minded sons of toil, so Mencken, Babbitt, Pound, Eliot, and the Agrarians assumed that they belonged to some sort of superior breed.

And just as many of the leftists condoned the use of force, so too the ultra-conservatives talked in terms of repressive methods. In *I'll Take My Stand* Allen Tate wrote: "We are very near an answer to our question— How may the Southerner take hold of his tradition? The answer is by violence." [71] In the same book Tate expressed the Agrarian views on Negroes:

> I argue it this way: the white race seems determined to rule the Negro in its midst; I belong to the white race; therefore I intend to support white rule. Lynching is a symptom of weak, inefficient rule; but you can't destroy lynching by *fiat* or social legislation; lynching will disappear when the white race is satisfied that its supremacy will not be questioned in social crises.[72]

T. S. Eliot's series of talks at the University of Virginia has already been cited. In addition to praising the Agrarians and deploring free-thinking Jews he stated that "a spirit of excessive tolerance is to be deprecated."

It is significant that these remarks were published in *The American Review* in 1934. Under the editorship of Seward Collins *The American Review* was enthusiastic about Agrarians, English Distributists (Pound's enthusiasm), Neo-Humanists, Christians as defined by Eliot, and fascists such as Sir Oswald Mosley and Mussolini. It published a series of articles by a lay Catholic professor advocating the creation in America of a fascist type of organization to purge politics and the press.

The fact that so many intellectuals on both the left and the right adopted extremist positions is probably due to certain fundamental flaws in their approach to life. On the one hand they tend to substitute theory for experience, on the other they tend to demand absolute or utopian solutions to social, economic, and political problems.

It is no accident that the one President of the twentieth century who could be described as primarily an intellectual did more than any other to loose upon the United States the forces of fanaticism. In his attempt to rally support for an undesired war, Wilson's propaganda machine under George Creel whipped up the emotions of Americans to hatred of the enemy. At home dissenters like Debs and Haywood were jailed. Debs drew a ten-year sentence; Haywood and other I. W. W. leaders got twenty years. Because of opposition to American entry into the War, *The Seven Arts* lost its financial support; and the editors of *The Masses* were tried for sedition. The Rand School of Social Science was fined $3000 for publishing a pamphlet critical of the War.

According to Samuel Eliot Morison and Henry Steele Commager, the Espionage Act of June 1917 and the Sedition Act of May 1918 "were as extreme as any legislation anywhere in the world." [73] These historians quoted Wilson's statement: "We are glad to fight for the privilege of men everywhere to choose their way of life—and of obedience," [74] and then added that "this exalted ideal did not apply to the United States."

When Germany surrendered, the hatreds and suspicions which had been whipped up turned on foreigners and dissenters, especially upon Socialists and members of the I. W. W. In 1919 the House of Representatives by a vote of 309 to 1 unseated the Socialist Representative,

Victor Berger of Milwaukee. Five Socialists elected to the New York Assembly were likewise denied their seats.[75] A revived Ku Klux Klan became politically powerful, not only in the South but in states like Indiana and Illinois. In Harrisburg, Pennsylvania, thousands of Klansmen gathered for a convention and put on a mile-long parade. Crosses burned on Northern hillsides. Wilson's Attorney-General, A. Mitchell Palmer, obtained warrants for the arrest of 6000 "dangerous aliens." [76] A total of 4000 were arrested and 1000 deported. Without warrants Palmer's agents broke into labor meetings, made arrests and seized documents. F. Scott Fitzgerald's story "May Day" gives a vivid picture of men and women at a plush Yale alumni party watching American Legionaires smash the offices of a Socialist newspaper. The business community's approval of the suppression of dissent is indicated by the fact that between 1919 and 1921 three institutions—Swarthmore College, Lafayette College, and George Washington University—gave Palmer honorary degrees. It is of course boards of trustees, not the faculty, who select the recipients of honorary degrees.

It was during Wilson's regime that a group of lawyers, headed by Charles Evans Hughes, issued a report declaring that "perhaps to an extent unparalleled in our history, the essentials of liberty are being disregarded. . . . We know of violations of personal rights which savor of the worst practices of tyranny." [77] It was Warren G. Harding who pardoned Debs.

This suppression of all dissent under Wilson is characteristic of the doctrinaire intellectual. Max Eastman, who was very critical of Wilson, took an equally intolerant stand in an article for *The Masses* of June 1917 in which he said that the Socialist Party should "unify its platform under the working principle that all changes which can be clearly proven to benefit labor *at the expense of capital* [Ital. mine] are socialistic. . . ." [78]

An editorial on Wilson by Walter E. Weyl in *The New Republic* for June 7, 1919 has larger implications: it points up one of the fatal weaknesses of the intellectual as a type:

> The simple faith of Mr. Wilson in his Fourteen Points, unexplained and unelaborated, was due, I believe, to the invincible abstractness of his mind. . . . In his political thinking and propaganda Mr. Wilson cuts away all the complex qualities which things possess in real life in order to fasten upon one single characteristic, and thus he creates a clear but over-simple and unreal formula.

Weyl went on to suggest that the Fourteen Points containing the doctrine of self-determination of peoples ignored the historic, geographic, and economic realities of Europe.

With the opening of the archives of the Central Powers scholars began to discover the secret agreements of the Allies to parcel out territory. Under the chairmanship of Gerald Nye a Senate committee revealed the part played by bankers and munitions makers in causing the war and bringing the United States into it. These things along with the punitive Versailles Treaty and the destruction of civil liberties at home made Wilson's slogan about a war to make the world safe for Democracy a kind of obscene mockery. It is cut from exactly the same cloth as the intellectual left's slogans about the People's Republic in Russia as opposed to American "imperialism." Just as Wilson refused to face the realities of European power politics, the leftists, as so many of them have since admitted, refused to see the brutal realities of Stalin's dictatorship.

The intellectual's occupational hazard of substituting theory or ideology for reality is partly due to the nature of his task, that of seeking amid the chaos of data some basic laws or principles. When some principle or law seems to emerge as it did to Marx, or for that matter to Beard, there is great temptation to neglect conflicting evidence and to force data into harmony with theory. This is especially the danger in the fields of political, economic, and social study where the data are multiform, constantly shifting, and not subject to empirical verification.

If anything emerges from this survey of the political views of intellectuals between 1910 and 1930 it is the doctrinaire quality of the discussion. By 1955 Max Eastman had come to recognize this fundamental weakness in left-wing thinking.

> . . . the basic error in the whole century-long blunder has been a crude and foolish conception, or no-conception, of human nature. The socialist idea was dreamed up by intellectual and radical-minded people, who constitute a very small and not typical section of the human race. You might almost describe the socialist movement as an effort of the intelligentsia to put over their tastes and interests upon the mass of mankind.[79]

The same charge could be made against the right-wing intellectuals. Irving Babbitt preached that people must develop the will to refrain, by which he seems to have meant to refrain from the desire for social justice. Over and over the Agrarians insisted that people must learn to want fewer goods; they must learn to prefer farms to wages. In other words they must conform to the pattern defined by an intellectual elite.

Unlike intellectuals such as Franklin, Madison, Hamilton, and Jefferson, those of the early twentieth century rarely had first-hand experience with the problems of government. Many of the founding fathers had served in state or national assemblies; they had held administrative offices. Most of the later intellectuals not only lacked such experience, they were often inferior to the founders in scholarly knowledge. The lawyers in the Constitutional Convention had cut their teeth on Coke and Blackstone—authorities who were cited in the debates over ratification. Men such as James Wilson, George Wythe, John Adams, Hamilton and especially Madison had read widely on the subject of government. To prepare himself for the Constitutional Convention Madison had asked Jefferson to send him books from France.[80] The books arrived by the hundreds: thirty-seven volumes of the new *Encyclopedia Methodique,* biographies, histories, memoirs, books on political theory and the law of nations. He arrived at the Convention with two horses, one which he rode, the other which had saddlebags full of books.

By contrast Woodrow Wilson as observed by Maynard Keynes at the peace conference

> . . . had thought out nothing; when it came to practice, his ideas were nebulous and incomplete. He had no plan, no scheme, no constructive ideas whatever for clothing with the flesh of life the commandments which he had thundered from the White House. . . .
>
> He not only had no proposals in detail, but he was in many respects, perhaps inevitably, ill informed as to European conditions.[81]

There can be little question of the basic idealism of Wilson's desire for a better world order. Possibly he faced an impossible task. But certainly during his second term he sacrificed democratic principles on the altar of an abstract ideal.

It seems clear that from the jettisoning of Progressivism after 1917 until the election of Franklin Roosevelt the voice of liberal democracy was nearly drowned out by the business community and by the intellectuals of the left and right. With the discrediting of banking and big business after 1929 it might seem that the left-wing intellectuals who had preached the evils of capitalism would come into their own.

However despite the howls of alarmed conservatives and the dire predictions of the leftists the United States did not become a socialist state nor a fascist dictatorship. Although there were left-wing intellectuals in the New Deal, its course was not that plotted by the intellectuals but by practical politicians in the White House, the Congress, and the state capitols. Its major policies: farm relief, cheaper money, a moratorium on mortgages, tighter governmental control of banking and the stock market, the encouragement of labor unionism, and the limitation of the power of the courts to grant injunctions and to strike down social legislation—all were inherited from the Populist, Progressive and labor movements of the period from 1890 to 1916. They were not policies based on abstract ideologies but were pragmatic measures growing out of native and popular movements.

The leftists had drawn their theories from Europe, from syndicalism, anarchism, from Marx and Lenin; the rightists had looked to aristocratic systems of the past or flirted with fascism. If the history of the United States after 1932 demonstrated anything, it revealed the tunnel-vision of the intellectuals. Left and right they had depicted the bankruptcy of democracy; they had preached revolution as the only solution. What happened was an evolutionary change within the framework of the Constitution so despised by the intellectuals—a series of adjustments and compromises of economic interests as predicted by Madison.

But I, despite expert advice,
Keep doing things I think are nice,
Although to good I never come—
Inseparable my nose and thumb.
                                    Dorothy Parker

5.

The Sophomores

Mencken's views on politics had a certain nose-thumbing quality which can justifiably be called sophomoric. It
is a quality which characterized much of the writing of
the era. Traditionally the sophomore is thought of as
brash, irreverent, lively, clever rather than wise, intellectually shallow but pretending to knowledge and sophistication, and with a penchant for shocking his grandmother.
This description better fits the college boy of the bulldog-
on-the-bank era than the student of today, who by his
second year is concerned with social justice or has his eye
on graduate school or possibly has both in mind. In criticism it is the difference between Henry Mencken and say
Lionel Trilling; in the novel between Sinclair Lewis and
William Faulkner; in poetry between E. E. Cummings and
Robert Lowell.

A number of Mencken's remarks already quoted illus-
trate the point. Many of them like his comments on Anglo-
Saxons, New England writers, clergymen, and govern-

mental officials were gaily irresponsible—more designed to shock than to be taken as serious judgments. For instance in the *Mercury* he remarked

> If the combined aim and object of art lies in the stirring of the emotions, and is praiseworthy, why should the similar aim and object of the vices be regarded as meritricious? If the Madonnas of Raphael, Holbein, Murillo and Da Vinci are commendable in that they stir the imagination, why are not the whiskies of Dewar, Macdonald, Haig and Macdougel commendable for the same reason? If a Bach fuge is praised for stimulating the mind, why not a Corona Corona? [1]

He enjoyed taking the role of the village atheist: "For a bishop to fall on his knees spontaneously and begin to pray to God would make almost as great a scandal as if he mounted his throne in a bathing suit." [2] In "Hint to Theologians" he pointed to "evidence of divine incompetence" in the design of the human body "magnificently designed in some details [and] a frightful botch in other details." [3] Perhaps the universe was run by a board of gods who mess up each other's designs.

As a theologian Ezra Pound was equally profound. The Lord had set man in a garden and commanded him to tend it . . . "but it would have been very difficult for Adam to cultivate a garden 3000 miles long. Perhaps he had helpers. . . ." Pound found it difficult to believe "that there was a tree which taught good and evil, as there are pear trees and peach trees." In any case why did God not wish man to know good from evil? Eve was not surprised when the serpent spoke to her: "Animals are always talking in the old stories." [4] After discussing Cain and Abel, Pound summed up the whole import of the Bible as:

. . . what appears to the wise of the world, contrary
to all justice, contrary to all common sense principles,
is that God has eternally damned the whole human
race, and has slaughtered his own son, quite uselessly
for an apple, and that he pardoned fratricide.[5]

Margaret Anderson said of Pound ten years later that
it would be interesting to know him "when he grows up." [6]
One is reminded of Sinclair Lewis standing in a funda-
mentalist pulpit and challenging God to strike him dead.
Edgar Lee Masters very properly put such philosophy into
the mouth of a village iconoclast:

The reason I believe God crucified His Own Son
To get out of the wretched tangle is, because it sounds
    just like him.

Even when Mencken attempted serious evaluations
he could not avoid the smart-alec tone. In arguing that
Christianity had little to do with the teachings of Christ,
he went on, "It is the invention of Paul and his attendant
rabble-rousers—a body of men exactly comparable to the
corps of evangelical pastors of to-day, which is to say, a body
devoid of sense and lamentably indifferent to common
honesty." [7]

Mencken's wit, so much celebrated in his own time,
often boils down to ingenious name calling: *rabble-rousers,
booboisie, Homo boobiens, Homo meandertalensis.* Less
imaginatively, the common people were peasants or mo-
rons; politicians were mountebanks; clergymen were witch
doctors. When he aimed at an obvious target like Bryan,
Harding, or Coolidge, he could be very funny, but he used
the same kind of ammunition against Theodore Roosevelt

and Wilson; he attacked social legislation and the League of Nations in the same tone that he used against Prohibition and Comstockery.

Unlike Swift who saw mankind as a miserable race of vermin, or Twain who talked about the damned human race, or Housman who thought that the world ailed from the prime foundation; Mencken viewed the scene from the standpoint of a fraternity-house cynic drinking beer with his cronies and laughing at the non-fraternity types in the Y. M. C. A.

As has been noted, the man often bracketed with Mencken in the literary vaudeville was Sinclair Lewis. Certainly they shared a kind of brashness and a tendency to show off. In comparing them Walter Lippmann suggested that Lewis was the more callow:

> The prophet of this metropolitan spirit, toward which Carol [Kennicott] reaches out, is Mr. Mencken. Now Mr. Mencken is a true metropolitan. Mr. Lewis is a half-baked metropolitan. He has just arrived in the big city. He has the new sophistication of one who is bursting to write to the folks back home and let them know what tremendous fellows we are who live in the great capitals. There is more than a touch of the ex-naif in Mr. Lewis. . . .
>
> The terrible judgments which he pronounces upon the provincial civilization of America flow from the bitterness of a revolted provincial.[8]

One may question the urbanity of Mr. Mencken; it seems much more a kind of beer-hall sophistication. Carol Kennicott is less its victim than is Sinclair Lewis. Her vision of the good life came from novels and from *House*

Beautiful rather than from the fraternity house and the bar room.

But Lippmann was right about the half-baked metropolitanism of Lewis. At Yale he had been made to feel very much the outsider, as he pointed out in a bitter speech after he became famous. His exposure to an Ivy League experience seems as unrelated to the man as does the college degree of George F. Babbitt to that moronic character. Certainly in *Main Street, Babbitt,* and especially *Elmer Gantry* he justified Alfred Kazin's phrase, "the garrulous village atheist." The words of Miles Bjornstam in *Main Street* could apply to Lewis himself: "I'm the town bad-man, Mrs. Kennicott: town atheist, and I suppose I must be an anarchist too. Everybody who doesn't love the bankers and the Grand Old Republican Party is an anarchist." He added that "The dollar sign has chased the crucifix clean off the map."

When he tried to be philosophical, Lewis tended to repeat the Populist formulas of thirty years earlier with an added dash of Mencken:

> Finally, behind all her comments, Carol saw the fact that the prairie towns no more exist to serve the farmers who are their reason for existence than do the great capitals; they exist to fatten on the farmers, to provide the townsmen with large motors and social preferment. . . . It is a parasitic Greek civilization—minus the civilization.

One of the things which give authenticity to a Lewis novel was his ability to identify with certain aspects of his protagonists even when he was satirizing other aspects —even at times to share the quality he was satirizing. Thus he could share Carol's revulsion at the ugliness and philistinism of the village, and at the same time recognize the prissiness of her response. He once admitted that he drew Babbitt as a partial portrait of himself. Certainly Sam Dodsworth's awed provincial response to Europe was very much that of Sinclair Lewis. Sam wonders:

> Why had he even gone abroad? It had unsettled him. He had been bored in Paris, yet he liked crepes suzettes better than flapjacks; he liked leaning over the bridges of the Seine better than walking on Sixth Avenue. . . . How was it that this America, which had been so surely and comfortably in his hand, had so slipped away?

As Grace Hegger Lewis said of their own experience in Europe, ". . . it was a tourist Paris we were to see in the company of English and Americans who had jobs and knew the 'ropes.' " She described Lewis as a man who loved his country deeply but who could not live there or anywhere else with contentment. Her reminiscences of Lewis in Europe include a number of incidents and ideas which he incorporated in *Dodsworth*. Lewis, like Sam, was very much the provincial discovering a more cosmopolitan world. It is this awed discovery that the novelist shares with his characters which helps to give his novels an adolescent quality.

This quality also appears in their style and structure. If he wanted to show that American men are given to the use of slang, he provided speeches for Dr. Kennicott and George Babbitt which are practically lexicons of supposedly current clichés of the American language. Even as late as 1929 he represented the president of the motor company—a facsimile of General Motors—which had bought out Dodsworth's company—as saying:

Europe? Rats! Dead's a dornail! Place for women and long-haired artists. Dead! Only American loans that keep 'em from burying the corpse! All this art! More art in a good shiny spark plug than in all the fat Venus de Mylos they ever turned out. Naw! Go take a run through California, maybe grab a drink of good liquor in Mexico, and then come with us. Look here, Dodsworth. My way of being diplomatic is to flat out. You necking around with some other concern?

When Sam hesitates, president Kynance goes on:

My god man, what do you think is the purpose of life? Loafing? Getting by with doing as little as you can? I tell you, what I always say is: there is no rest like a little extra work! You ain't tried—you're just fed up with this backwoods town. Come up to Detroit and see how we make things hum! Come sit in with us and hear us tell Congress where it gets off. Work! That's the caper! . . . Do big things! Think of it, by making autos we're enabling half the civilized world to run into town from their pig-sties and see the movies, and the other half to get out of town and give Nature the once-over.

One may be permitted to wonder if the critics of the twenties were accurate in hailing the phonographic realism of Lewis. On the whole *Dodsworth* was an attempt at serious discussion, even if much of the conversation and comment has a fraternity-house naive earnestness. When Lewis was primarily satiric, as in *The Man Who Knew Coolidge,* he could represent a businessman who had been to Amherst, if only briefly, as describing his talk on birth control to the Zenith Chamber of Commerce:

"Shucks, boys," I said, "you know just as much about it as I do," but they talked and insisted, and they wouldn't let me go until I'd made a long spiel for 'em, summing up the arguments on both sides and, you might say, kind of clarifying it for 'em. See how I mean? But you, Walt, you must just think of business night and day, and prob'ly a more practical way to think of it. But I get dragged into all these public and influential occasions and get into a habit of oratory and philosophy, see how I mean?

On scores of occasions George F. Babbitt delivers himself of a similar mixture of modern and antiquated usage, the expression of equally muddle-headed opinions. In fact whole slabs of dialogue could be transferred without change from Will Kennicott to George Babbitt, to Lowell Schmaltz and to a variety of minor characters. They all blend into the booboisie of H. L. Mencken as reflected in his *Americana* column.

Like the endless parody of American speech is the obvious device which Lewis worked over and over of having a character present contradictory opinions within a few sentences. Thus when Carol Kennicott asks her husband if there is not a lot of jealousy and enmity among physicians, he indignantly denies it, then goes on for several paragraphs to express his own jaundiced views of his professional rivals. Lowell Schmaltz after speaking in favor of prohibition immediately proceeds to tell of his visit to a New York speakeasy where his WCTU wife ordered a Manhattan cocktail.

In his early novels Lewis could write vividly, often sensitively of a small-town drug store, of farm women in wagons waiting outside saloons for their drunken husbands, of a midwestern autumn landscape, even of the inchoate aesthetic longings of George F. Babbitt. In all his novels of the 1920s there is a vague idealism, desire for a more beautiful and civilized America; one as in *Arrowsmith* where service is more than a word, science more than an electric dishwasher; or as in *Dodsworth* where the European idea of good food and conversation prevails. Like Carol Kennicott, Lewis had a sentimental sympathy with those seeking social justice. Yet in all these areas Lewis rarely went beyond the undergraduate questionings and sympathies of Fitzgerald's Amory Blaine of *This Side of Paradise*.

The limitations of Lewis as a writer may in part account for the huge sale of his novels—140,000 for *Main Street* alone. The ideas expressed put no great strain upon the reader who, if he was at all a sensitive person, had also been repelled by some of the more obvious crudities of manners, advertising, business, and evangelical religion. Lewis' bold colors and slap-dash style made it easy for the most casual reader to get the point of any incident, to understand every character.

Even the kinds of people caricatured could say to themselves, "I may use some of those expressions, but I don't talk like that," or "I'm not as dumb as all that." It is a device as old as Plautus to represent a stupid fellow or a hypocrite in such exaggerated terms that their counterparts in the audience will not be offended; they can feel smugly superior to the fictional character. On the other hand the intellectuals, conditioned by the cultural wasteland doctrines of Henry James, Henry Adams, Van Wyck Brooks, H. L. Mencken, and the Ivy League professors, were quite ready to accept Lewis' portrait of America, especially of midwestern America as authentic. Edith Wharton, always on the lookout for American vulgarities, told Lewis that *Main Street* revealed a midwest of which she knew nothing. Obviously her midwestern characters in *The Custom of the Country* and *Hudson River Bracketed* are not drawn so much from life as from the novels of Lewis.

Another reason for the popularity of *Main Street* was that a considerable number of Americans were themselves escapees from the village, often by way of college. Between 1900 and 1920 the percentage of the urban population of the United States rose from 39 to 51.4. More significant perhaps, from a literary standpoint, the percentage of Americans going to college more than doubled. As dozens of novels of college life testify, the collegiate experience often involved at least a temporary rejection of traditional values. To the young the home folks looked like old fogies, especially in an era of accelerated social change. This helps to explain the frequently adolescent quality of the revolt. H. L. Mencken and Sinclair Lewis were particular heroes of the younger generation. An elderly professor at the University of Chicago spoke for his generation when he said, "The one thing that makes me fear for the future is the number of our students who read the *American Mercury;* on the campus you see it under every arm; they absorb everything in it." [9]

Mencken and Lewis were not of the jazz-age generation, but the youngsters found in their work useful testimony against their elders. As has been noted, Mencken detested jazz. Grace Lewis said that in Europe her husband did not join the Riviera crowd of the Fitzgeralds; in fact "the Jazz Age had not the slightest interest for Lewis." [10] To a much greater degree than the nose-thumbing Mencken, Lewis was a serious social critic; in his naive way he was searching for values beyond those of Main Street and Zenith. Whatever their artistic faults, *Arrowsmith* and *Dodsworth* depict Americans in search of an identity beyond that as members of a crass society. But *Elmer Gantry* and *The Man Who Knew Coolidge* (1928) might seem the intemperate work of an angry young man despite the fact that Lewis was in his forties when he wrote them. No one today could regard them as the work of a mature literary artist.

The writer who impressed his contemporaries as a mature artist was James Branch Cabell. The critical tributes to him by Mencken, Canby, and Carl Van Doren have been cited in an earlier chapter.

The undergraduates instinctively knew better. They may have been taken in by Cabell's rococo style but they recognized that *Jurgen* was a locker-room epic disguised as mythology. Parts of it are indeed amusing; the sophomore could snicker over the account of Jurgen teaching mathematics to the Queen, an ingenious reworking of classic farm-boy and travelling salesmen stories. The numerous phallic references to spears with red tips, to swords and sheaths, to torn veils required no knowledge of Frazer or Jessie Weston. *Jurgen* is in many ways more adolescent than *Fanny Hill,* for instead of treating sex openly it conceals pornographic drawings in an allegedly innocent landscape. In his defense of the novel against obscenity Cabell took refuge in the oh-what-a-dirty-mind-you-have argument, a favorite theme of jokes in the college humor magazines of the twenties.

A recurrent theme in the novel is one that re-echoed during the period:

> All men that live have but a little while to live, and none knows his fate thereafter. So a man possesses nothing certainly save the brief loan of his own body; and yet the body of man is capable of much curious pleasure.

This *carpe diem* theme is of course as old as literature but it is especially popular in periods of disillusion with the contemporary world. Thus it appears in a less sexy form in Arnold's *Dover Beach* and in Fitzgerald's reworking of the *Rubaiyat*. The 1890s decorated it with pale lost lilies and athletes dying young. The 1920s equated it specifically with sexual experience.

But between 1910 and 1920 there was an important shift in attitude. After the languors of the nineties and before the disillusion after the great war, sexual freedom was a cause. It was to be a part of a brave new world. Margaret Sanger campaigned for birth control not as an aid to promiscuity but as a means to promote happier marriage. Sex was something to be enjoyed frankly but as a part of a full and responsible life. In England Havelock Ellis and Marie Stopes preached similar doctrine. Even the proponents of free love argued that it was part of the full life. This was the theme of Floyd Dell's preaching in *The Masses* and *The Little Review*.

In the latter magazine for 1915 its editor, Margaret Anderson, charged that "false ideas of sex gave us the hard, tight, anaemic, metallic woman who flourishes in America as nowhere else." [11] Something of the pre-war attitude remains in Dell's *Intellectual Vagabondage* (1926) in which he expressed the hope that a younger generation would "begin to formulate and erect into socially acceptable *conventions,* and where possible into laws, some healthy modern ideals of courtship, marriage, divorce, and the relations between the sexes in general." [12]

This is rather different from the flapper philosophy celebrated by Edna St. Vincent Millay who opened her volume *A Few Figs from Thistles* with the famous quatrain about the lovely light given off by burning her candle at both ends. (The popular song "Smoke Gets in My Eyes" belongs to a later and sadder decade.) Along with F. Scott Fitzgerald, Miss Millay became one of the chief voices of the Jazz Age. Like Dorothy Parker she thumbed her nose at prudent counsel. In *A Few Figs from Thistles* she wrote contemptuously of the allegedly ugly houses safe upon the solid rock, and invited everyone to see her shining palace built upon the sand. One is reminded of Gatsby's dream mansion. Like Fitzgerald she took the view:

> The years that Time takes off my life,
> He'll take from off the other end.

In *Rivers to the Sea* (1915) Sara Teasdale had sung of the quick passing of love. The annual return of roses burning at the door brought the reflection

> Strange so frail a flame outlasts
> Fire in the heart.

The theme, like the imagery, has been around for a long time.

What Millay did with it was to introduce the flapper sensibility of the era, a time when girls prided themselves on being "hard-boiled." Thus in "Thursday" Millay derided a lover who complained of being loved on Wednesday and discarded on Thursday.

> I loved you Wednesday—yes—but what
> Is that to me.

She advised a lover:

> I shall forget you presently, my dear,
> So make the most of this your little day . . .

One remembers Daisy Buchanan's remark to Nick Carraway, "Sophisticated—God, I'm sophisticated." Like Daisy, Miss Millay could also play the oh-the-pain-of-it song:

> I cannot say what loves have come and gone;
> I only know that summer sang in me
> A little while, that in me sings no more.

Edmund Wilson may be right in arguing that Edna St. Vincent Millay has been underestimated in recent years. Her technical skill was impressive; her gift of phrase superior to that of many of her contemporaries. Like very different poets such as Masters, Sandburg, Lindsay, and even Frost she was eclipsed by the success of Eliot and his followers in poetry and criticism. The point of the present discussion is that much of her work in the 1920s, especially *A Few Figs from Thistles,* presented a sophomoric view of love and life. This becomes especially obvious when her work is compared to that of Emily Dickinson. The earlier poet could write far more intensely of love and death:

> I could not die with you,
> For one must wait
> To shut the other's gaze down—
> You could not.

And I, could I stand by
And see you freeze,
Without the right of frost,
Death's privilege?

Nor could I rise with you,
Because Your face
Would put out Jesus;
That new grace.

Perhaps without realizing it Emily Dickinson belonged to the tradition of Donne who used daring metaphor and hyperbole to record intensity of feeling, such as his assertion that a lock of his love's hair could be viceroy for his departed soul and keep his limbs from dissolution or that the worlds found by sea discoverers were inconsequential compared to the one world he and his love have found.

Millay is more in the adolescent tradition of Housman and Dowson, the one mourning that of "threescore years and ten, Twenty will not come again," and the other talking about flinging roses riotously with the throng. Her plaint that "summer sang in me a little while, that in me sings no more," echoes Housman, and her lines:

So wanton, light and false my love, are you,
I am most faithless when I am most true,

suggest "I have been faithful to thee Cynara in my fashion."

Perhaps not a line that Millay wrote has the probing impact of Dickinson's "I like a look of agony, Because I know it's true;"

Millay's contemporary, E. E. Cummings, was a more original but often a somewhat sophomoric poet. His eccentric form, continued throughout his life, is obviously a revolt against the precepts of his elders. At his best Cummings could use the form functionally as in "Just spring" where the odd spacing of the lines and syllables indicates the timing of the music—of the held breath of the children, then the sudden rush of eddieandbill to the mud-luscious outdoors where the

> goat-footed
> baloonMan whistles
> far
> and
> wee

He could write superb love lyrics like "somewhere i have never travelled" which contains the lines

> your slightest look will easily unclose me . . .
>
> nothing which we are to perceive in his world
> equals the power of your intense fragility;
> whose texture compels me with the colour of
> its countries, rendering death and forever
> with each breathing . . . nobody, not even
> the rain, has such small hands.

But a considerable amount of Cummings' verse is light-hearted horsing around like "nobody loses all the time" about Uncle Sol who failed at running a chicken farm, a skunk farm, and at trying to drown himself, but finally died "and started a worm farm." This is not to deplore the fact that the man who could write some of the most sensitive lyrics of the era should also have turned his hand to satire. Rather it is a lament that so talented a poet should have devoted so much of his time to Dadaistic doodling such as the considerable number of poems which consist largely of odd arrangements of letters and punctuation marks like this ending:

```
           s:
             A
           V
           o(
           .
           :
           ;
           ,
```

He could include in a volume of serious poetry the bawdy "may i feel said he"—a detailed, light hearted account of seduction.

More important is the fact that Cummings never really matured. There is little to distinguish the poetry he wrote at fifty from his work at tweny-five. Oscar Cargill, who failed to recognize the best work, was almost right in saying, "The naughty boy, the sophomore, the undeveloped mind in Cummings is very tedious." [13] Like Mencken and Lewis, Cummings is most interesting in excerpts. Like Edna St. Vincent Millay he leaves the mature reader with the impression of talent and youthfulness.

Youth and the adventures of youth have been an enduring theme in the novel from Fielding to Salinger.

R. W. B. Lewis has shown that the American Adam, the innocent facing a corrupt society, is an important archetype in our literature. But during the period under consideration another youthful archetype became common in fiction—that of the American Ariel. It will be remembered that Ariel was a poet and singer with a longing to be free and a lack of lasting human affections. During the second renaissance he appeared as Felix Fay in Dell's *The Moon Calf;* as Eugene Witla in Dreiser's *The Genius;* as Gareth Johns in Van Vechten's *The Tattooed Countess;* and in feminine form as Thea Kronborg in Willa Cather's *The Song of the Lark.* Wolfe's George Webber in *The Web and the Rock* is a later version of the same character, but the novel has been shown to be a record of Wolfe's experiences and emotional life between 1925 and 1928.[14]

What these characters have in common is that all of them leave prosaic homes, abandon early lovers, and seek freedom and self-expression with considerable ruthlessness. The type is not exclusively American, but its ubiquity during the period under discussion suggests that it represented an important element in the *Zeitgeist.* By and large this was a generation of spiritual expatriates from the values of their parents, from early comrades and girl friends; of necessity these writers often had to be somewhat ruthless with those who demanded old loyalties.

This cutting of roots is characteristically a phase of adolescence and young adulthood; it often happens during the college years. It is not surprising then that many of the novels of the period represent a sophomoric sensibility. This is of course artistically valid; it gives verisimilitude to youthful characters. It is a quality which gives vitality to such an amateurish novel as *This Side of Paradise.* However it is one thing to represent an immature character as thinking and feeling in an adolescent way; it is something else when the novelist shares this attitude—when the thoughts and emotions of the characters seem to reflect those of the writer.

Thus in his somewhat autobiographical novel, *The Genius,* the forty-four-year-old Dreiser clearly sympathizes with Eugene Witla's alleged "intense sense of beauty" which leads him to abandon his wife Angela and to pursue other women. "He and Angela were chance acquaintances —chemical affinities—never to meet again in all time. He and Christiana, he and Ruby—he and anyone—a few bright hours were all they could have together, and then would come the great silence, dissolution, and he would never be anyone."

In a less maudlin fashion the youthful Felix Fay spouts ideas which closely resemble those of the author, who was thirty-four when *The Moon Calf* was published. Dell represents the young man as telling his girl such things as:

> "I don't believe in most of the things other people believe in . . ."

> "And I don't believe in the conventional ideas of marriage."

He tells her: "I don't want you to be 'faithful' to me," he said with a contemptuous emphasis on the word. "I want you to be faithful to your own soul. . . ." Iconoclastic ideas are of course not necessarily sophomoric, but certainly Felix Fay's statements have an adolescent quality.

It is this quality which makes some of Sherwood Anderson's writing so embarrassing. *Winesburg, Ohio* seems like the work of a mature writer who has seen below the surface of a variety of lives; *Dark Laughter,* six years later, might have been written by a beginner. It is the story of John Stockton, a newspaper reporter, who walks out on his wife to go in search of himself. Taking the name of Bruce Dudley he tries to repeat Huck Finn's journey down the Mississippi. When he gets to New Orleans, he rents a cheap room where he spends much of his time in daydreaming, particularly about the life of Negroes. He envies their laughter, their easy morals, and imagines himself making love to the handsome Negro girl whose window he can look into. Later he goes north and gets a job varnishing automobile wheels but continues to live in a kind of daydream until the wife of the factory owner takes a fancy to him. In a diluted version of the Lady Chatterly story they have a brief affair, then run away together leaving Aline's nice but rather sexless husband in tears.

Now this is not the story of a youth but that of a thirty-four-year-old man whose emotional and intellectual life is that of a retarded adolescent. Anderson himself was forty-nine when he published the book. Yet he represents the twenty-nine year old Aline musing in her garden:

> Now was the time for her lover to come—to spring out of the ground—to drop from the branches of a tree—to take her, laughing at the very notion of consent.

Throughout the book Anderson delivers himself of such observations as:

> Flesh is flesh, a tree is a tree, grass is grass. The flesh of women is the flesh of trees, of flowers, of grasses.

Or again:

> Women are strange. No man ever finds out much about them.

One is reminded of the conversations between Fitzgerald's Amory Blaine and Burne Holiday:

> "How about religion?" Amory asked him.
> "Don't know. I'm in a muddle about a lot of things —I've just discovered that I've a mind, and I'm starting to read."
> "Read what?"
> "Everything. I have to pick and choose, of course, but mostly things to make one think."

Much of Fitzgerald's writing shows this intellectual muddle, this eclectic picking up of ideas. As for Amory there is the conflict between puritanism and hedonism, between a vague longing for social justice and the attractions of wealth—conflicts which concerned Fitzgerald long after *This Side of Paradise*.

Blaine's attitude toward women shows the characteristic ambivalence of the undergraduate: they are both bitches and dream girls. Rosalind of *This Side of Paradise*, Gloria Gilbert of *The Beautiful and Damned*, Daisy Buchanan of *The Great Gatsby* are all vain and selfish and shallow; but they are gloriously beautiful and desirable. Thus of Gloria:

> She was dazzling—alight; it was agony to comprehend her beauty in a glance. Her hair, full of a heavenly glamour, was gay against the winter color of the room.

Or again:

> Surely the freshness of her cheeks was a gossamer projection from a land of delicate and undiscovered shades; her hand gleaming on the stained table-cloth was a shell from some far and wildly virginal sea. . . .

In the story *Winter Dreams,* Dexter loses Judy Jones to a richer man. Ten years later, hearing that her beauty has faded, he indulges in a reverie worthy of Edna St. Vincent Millay:

> The dream was gone . . .
> For the first time in years the tears were streaming down his face. But they were for himself now. He did not care about mouth and eyes and moving hands. He wanted to care, and he could not care. For he had gone away and he could never go back any more. The gates were closed, the sun was gone down, and there was no beauty but the gray beauty of steel that withstands all time. Even the grief he could have borne was left behind in the country of illusion, of youth, of the richness of life, where his winter dreams had flourished.

What makes Fitzgerald's glamorizing tolerable is his awareness of the difference between the dream and the reality. This same Judy, who falls in and out of love overnight, is described thus:

> She was entertained only by the gratification of her desires and by the direct exercise of her own charm. Perhaps from so much youthful love, so many youthful lovers, she had come, in self-defence, to nourish herself wholly from within.

And of Gloria Gilbert at twenty-nine:

> She knew in her breast she had never wanted chil-
> dren. The reality, the earthiness, the intolerable senti-
> ment of child-bearing, the menace to her beauty—had
> appalled her. She wanted to exist only as a conscious
> flower, prolonging and preserving itself.

After Gatsby is murdered because he chivalrously con-
cealed the fact that Daisy drove the death car,

> They were careless people, Tom and Daisy—they
> smashed things and creatures and then retreated back
> into their money or their vast carelessness, or what-
> ever it was that kept them together, and let other
> people clean up the mess they had made. . . .

Nevertheless the charm of Jay Gatsby is that he had preserved his adolescent ideal of Daisy as the dream girl. He
is crooked; he is often ridiculous, but Fitzgerald obviously
shares Nick Carraway's view of Gatsby: "You're worth the
whole damn bunch put together." In the last scene Carraway (Fitzgerald) musing on Gatsby's sense of wonder at the
first sight of the green light at the end of Daisy's dock
suddenly shifts to the plural; he identifies with Gatsby's
emotion:

> Gatsby believed in the green light, the orgiastic
> future that year by year recedes before us. It eluded
> us then, but that's no matter—tomorrow we will run
> faster, stretch out our arms farther. . . . And one
> fine morning—

It is significant that this, one of the three or four best novels of its decade, should have as its tragic protagonist a man with an adolescent dream.

Dick Diver in *Tender is the Night* is equally adolescent but without Gatsby's odd attractiveness. In one version of the novel we first meet Dick dressed in a pair of lace panties made by his wife Nicole. Dick is supposedly a psychiatrist who has spent "eight years teaching the rich the ABC's of human decency," yet throughout much of the novel he engages in the same kind of undergraduate antics for which Fitzgerald became notorious. In fact some of the incidents like the drunken fight with the taxi driver are autobiographical. Dick's affair with Rosemary is equally immature: she is a beautiful, childish movie star.

This is not the place to analyze the structure of the novel, a problem Fitzgerald never solved to his own satisfaction. The point at issue is that all the chief characters except the sinister Baby Warren are essentially immature, and their tragedies grow out of the immaturity of their emotions and behavior. Dick and Nicole Diver are so obviously patterned on Scott and Zelda Fitzgerald that there is justification for attributing to the writer the immaturity of his fictional characters.

More important, Fitzgerald's sensibility as revealed in both novels and short stories is essentially sophomoric. Character after character bemoans the approach of his thirtieth birthday. Fitzgerald himself set a date for suicide at thirty but later advanced it. In the person of Charlie Wales in *Babylon Revisited* (1931) Fitzgerald wrote:

His first feeling was one of awe that he had actually, in his mature years, stolen a tricycle and pedalled Loraine all over the Etoile between the small hours and dawn. . . . How many weeks or months of dissipation to arrive at that condition of utter irresponsibility?

Not only in life but in American literature the sophomore prom was over.

As with Fitzgerald it is difficult to separate Ernest Hemingway, the man from Hemingway, the writer. Just as Byron created the characters of Childe Harold, Selim of *The Bride of Abydos,* Manfred, and Don Juan out of projections of certain aspects of his own character, so Fitzgerald's handsome, romantic, and damned lovers are recognizable as Zelda and himself. So too Hemingway's Nick Adams, Frederick Henry, Harry of *The Snows of Kilimanjaro,* and to some degree Robert Jordan are all dramatizations of Ernest Hemingway. Fitzgerald created his characters out of his own legend; Hemingway tried to live up to the legend he had created. Carlos Baker's biography shows the considerable extent to which Hemingway embroidered the facts to create the legend.[15]

Thus Ernest's account of the poverty he endured in Paris while he was struggling to write is highly exaggerated; his wife Hadley had a moderate private income. But his dedication as an artist was genuine. His statement of what he was trying to do has become famous: to write prose "without tricks and without cheating." A writer, he said, must have talent, but there must be discipline: "The discipline of Flaubert"; there must be "an absolute conscience as unchanging as the standard meter in Paris, to prevent faking." When Fitzgerald wrote shoddy stuff, he did it for money; when Hemingway began to parody himself, it seems to have been because he had nothing new to say. He became like the fading bull fighter, Manuel Garcia, in *The Undefeated*—a man who would not quit but was too old for the game.

There is no disputing the excellence of Hemingway's early work. Even in a short story like *The Big Two Hearted River* he achieved the fourth or fifth dimension which he demanded of good prose—those symbolic meanings beyond the mere surface narrative. This is not so much the obvious kind of symbolism so beloved of academic critics—for instance Baker's attempt to show that in *A Farewell to Arms* the mountain represents the good life, the plain the corrupt life.* [16] At its best Hemingway's symbolism is the objective correlative of a state of mind or feeling like that of the well lighted cafe in *A Clean Well Lighted Place*. Often it is not even so clearly a one-to-one correlation as in that story; it may be a rendering through characters and events of a mood or feeling. The impotence of Jake Barnes has obviously a direct symbol-to-meaning relationship, but the whole of *The Sun Also Rises* is a complex interrelationship between people, scenes, and events to represent the psycopathology of an era. Although it has obvious parallels to Eliot's *The Waste Land, The Sun Also Rises* is in some ways a more subtle piece of work. The romantic and exasperating Robert Cohn and the bitchy and conflicted Lady Brett Ashley are more complex than the bored lover and lady in Eliot's "A Game of Chess." The final four sentences of the novel have more impact than any *Waste Land* passage of similar length:

"Oh Jake," Brett said, "we could have had such a good time together."

Ahead was a mounted policeman in khaki directing traffic. He raised his baton. The car slowed suddenly pressing Brett against me.

"Yes," I said, "Isn't it pretty to think so."

* This explication ignores the fact that Lieutenant Henry speaks of the good life he and Catherine had in Milan (on the plain): whereas there are numerous references to the ugly fighting in the mountains.

Nevertheless there is considerable justice in Alfred Kazin's statement that Hemingway "brought a major art to a minor vision of life." [17] What Kazin had in mind seems to have been Hemingway's nihilism and his preoccupation with violence and death. In many ways that vision was the result of the meaningless slaughter of World War I—a context in which the "separate peace" of Nick Adams made sense. As Lieutenant Henry says:

> I was always embarrassed by the words sacred, glorious, and sacrifice. . . . I had seen nothing sacred and the things that were glorious had no glory and the sacrifices were like the stockyards at Chicago if nothing was done with the meat except to bury it.

Like his alter-ego in *The Snows of Kilimanjaro* Hemingway "had seen things that he could never think of and later still he had seen much worse. . . ."

Where Hemingway's vision of life becomes embarrassing is in his attempts to be philosophical. Over and over he or one of his alter-egos delivers himself of such remarks as:

> Nobody ever lives their life all the way up except bull-fighters.
>
> *The Sun Also Rises*

> If people bring so much courage to this world the world has to break them, so of course it kills them.
>
> *A Farewell to Arms*

> "Madam, there is no remedy for anything in life."
>
> *Death in the Afternoon*

What did he fear? It was not fear or dread. It was a nothing that he knew too well. It was all a nothing and man was a nothing too. It was only that and light was all it needed and a certain cleanness and order . . . he knew it all was nada y pues nada y nada y pues nada. Our nada who are in nada, nada be thy name thy kingdom nada thy will be nada in nada as it is in nada. Give us this nada our daily nada, etc.

A Clean Well Lighted Place

What sets this last apart from the similar pessimism of *Ecclesiastes* is its tone. The Preacher who says, "I have seen all the works that are done under the sun; and behold all is vanity and vexation of spirit," is as disillusioned as Hemingway, but he's not thumbing his nose nor putting on a tough-guy prose.

The feeling that Hemingway's toughness, like Byron's world weariness, was partly a pose has disturbed many of his critics. There is more than a little point to Max Eastman's jibe about the literary fashion of wearing false hair on the chest. Obviously Hemingway was a sensitive man deeply wounded by the barbarities of life. In fact this might be stated as the major theme of his work.

This valid, even noble, theme is too often contaminated by the pose—the "Look I can take it" rejoinder which shades over into the "You never touched me" boast. Thus Lieutenant Henry, wounded as was Hemingway by shrapnel in the leg, constantly insists that he is OK even when the surgeons are probing. He boasts about his lack of a temperature; he demands that Catherine Barkley come to bed with him despite her insistence that it would not be good for him. Henry's wounds are so clearly Hemingway's that often they are physically and emotionally the same person. Like Lieutenant Henry, Hemingway wore his purple heart on his sleeve.

By contrast there was Oliver Wendell Holmes, Jr., wounded three times in the Civil War—once nearly dying of a shot through the neck—who remembered his war years as a time when "our hearts were touched with fire." Perhaps Holmes was as cynical about human motives as was Hemingway, but instead of parading his wound he went on to try to implement the Declaration of Independence and the Constitution, whereas Hemingway, nursing his wound, said in *The Green Hills of Africa* that he was through serving time "for society, democracy and the other things." As Philip Young has pointed out, ". . . Hemingway has, since 1924, been writing out the story of one man who is based on himself." [18]

Hemingway's identification with his fictional hero justifies the feeling that Lieutenant Henry's sexual exploits are meant to suggest those of the writer. Before he fell in love with Catherine, Henry went to the whorehouse every night; after Catherine became his mistress, he got her into his hospital bed night and morning. One is unpleasantly reminded of the aging Hemingway boasting to A. E. Hotchner that he was currently father of an African child and that he had laid Mata Hari, a woman who had been executed before he reached Europe. Baker quotes him as boasting that he had had every woman he ever wanted and some he didn't.

This sophomoric celebration of sexual exploits is related to Hemingway's faternity-house view of woman as either bitch or bedfellow—sometimes both. Lady Brett Ashley is clearly both; Mrs. Macomber is simply bitch who taunts her husband about her infidelities; Catherine Barkley and Maria of the sleeping bag are little more than bedmates. It is not unfair to identify the attitudes of Harry with those of Hemingway, for as Philip Young says "Harry is very autobiographically drawn. . . ." In the story Harry's wife "had a pleasant body [and] a great talent and appreciation for the bed." But for Harry, "Love is a dung-hill . . . and I'm the cock that gets on it to crow." He refers to his wife as a "rich bitch."

She says to him:

> "You don't have to destroy me. Do you? I'm only a middle-aged woman who loves you and wants to do what you want to do. I've been destroyed two or three times already. You wouldn't want to destroy me again, would you?"
>
> "I'd like to destroy you a few times in bed," he said.
>
> "Yes, that's the good destruction. That's the way we're made to be destroyed."

The exchanges between Harry and his wife are a kind of epitome of Hemingway's view of women and love.

What sets Hemingway apart from the other writers discussed in this chapter is that at his best he tried to deal with one of the themes of great literature: man in conflict with fate or the gods. Dreiser, Mencken, Lewis, and Fitzgerald were essentially concerned with man in social situations; the villains or scapegoats were the Puritan, the Philistine, the very rich. Hemingway was of course also concerned with what society did to the individual but there is an added dimension. Nick Adams, Jake Barnes, and Lieutenant Henry all had to cope with what Pound called "a botched civilization an old bitch gone in the teeth." But each had also to cope with "the blind fury with abhorred shears"—with chance and death. Henry was wounded not in battle but while sitting at mess; Catherine Barkley's death in childbirth had nothing to do with the war or human error; Harry died because a minor injury led to gangrene and the breakdown of a motor truck kept him from medical aid.

Hemingway's famous answer to the apparent meaninglessness of the universe was to exhibit grace under pressure. It was the code of his soldiers and bullfighters. It may not be a profound reading of life, but it has dignity. What too often sullied it was Hemingway's sophomoric pose as a Tarzan, his thinly-veiled boasting about his expertise on fishing, hunting and bull fighting, about his prowess in bed.

6.

Miniver Cheevy Rides Rosinante

In their crusade against American culture the iconoclasts naturally leveled their lances at two characteristic
features of it: science and technology. The term *technology* will be used here to include both the machine and
the industrial organization based upon it. A variety of
psychological motivations lay behind the attack by the
intellectuals. There was the heritage from Romantic literature: Blake's "dark satanic mills"; Rousseau's noble savage,
and Wordsworth's picturesque peasant; the medieval craftsman of Ruskin and Morris; the aestheticism of the eighties
and nineties. There was more than a hint of aristocratic
distaste for the urban proletariat. There was also the
natural antipathy of the scholar and writer for noise and
confusion: the factory and the railroad yards were getting
too close to the study. And for a number of writers there
was a nostalgia for the America of Grandma Moses.

As a rule, the crusade was more against technology
than against scientific thought; but the New Humanists and

the Agrarians included science in their demonology. The New Humanists were hostile to science because it contradicted what Norman Foerster, echoing Irving Babbitt, called the "central assumption of Humanism . . . the dualism of man and nature." [1] Bryan took with him to Dayton an anti-evolution book by Louis Trenchard More, the brother of Paul Elmer More.[2] Joseph Wood Krutch in *The Modern Temper* praised Hulme and Eliot, and as they did, lamented the breakdown of Medieval religious unity—a breakdown due, he claimed, to the invasion of science.[3]

On the other hand many of the writers of the second renaissance seized upon one or another of the teachings of social science or psychology. Freudian theory was used to support the attack on technology. The machine was alleged to be repressive of man's natural instincts. Yet it was Freud himself, in his *General Introduction to Psychoanalysis* (1920), who argued that the nostalgic yearning for an unspoiled landscape, to enjoy "freedom from the grip of the external world" was in "the mental domain of phantasy." [4] In *The Machine in The Garden* Leo Marx has traced the persistence of the pastoral fable in American literature from Irving to Fitzgerald. Obviously *Walden* is a central document.

It is significant that the revival of interest in Thoreau began in the 1920s. In *The Golden Day* (1926) Lewis Mumford contrasted the pioneer's attitude toward nature with Thoreau's. The one concerned himself with "extraneous necessities"; the other sought beauty and meaning:

What Thoreau left behind is still precious; men may still go out and make over America in the image of Thoreau.[5]

That this remaking of America would involve a turning away from technology is suggested by the comment:

> In Thoreau's time, industrialism had begun to puff itself up over its multiplication of goods and the increase of wants that it fostered, in order to provide the machine with an outlet for its ever-too-plentiful supply.[6]

The statement is typical of its period with the personification of industrialism and the machine as Frankenstein monsters. If instead of the phrase "multiplication of goods," he had mentioned sewing machines, corn shellers, reapers, and fire engines, the connotations would have been quite different. It was not the industrialism or the demands of the machine which caused the farmer of Thoreau's day to buy a patent churn or to hire a threshing machine; it was the weary arms of his wife and himself. It was not unnecessary goods which Thoreau saw on the freight cars of the Fitchburg railroad near his pond; he listed Maine lumber, Thomaston lime, bales of rags for the paper mill, Spanish hides, and salt fish reminding him of the Grand Banks. Like his spiritual descendants Thoreau was ambivalent about the machine. On the one hand he said that "We do not ride upon the railroad; it rides upon us"; on the other:

> I am refreshed and expanded when the freight train rattles past me, and I smell the stores which go dispensing their odours all the way from Long Wharf to Lake Champlain, reminding me of foreign parts of coral reefs, the Indian oceans, and tropical climes, and the extent of the globe.

Sherwood Anderson, a more mixed-up person, tried to link the tragic lives of his Winesburg characters to the evils of the machine age. Thus in the story "Godliness," Jesse Bentley, obsessed with a pre-industrial rural religion, prays: "O God, create in me another Jesse like that of old, to rule over men and to be the father of sons who shall be rulers." Disappointed that his only child is a girl, he sees in his grandson David the one who will fulfill his dream. In a scene in the woods the old man's obsession scares the child so much that he throws a stone at his grandfather. The story has nothing to do with industrialism but Anderson drags it in:

> He [Jesse] had grown into maturity in the years after the Civil War and he, like all men of his time had been touched by the deep influences that were at work in the country during those years when modern industrialism was being born. He began to buy machinery that would permit him to do the work of the farms while employing fewer men and he sometimes thought that if he were a younger man he would give up farming altogether and start a factory in Winesburg for the making of machinery.

Jesse's daughter, whose upbringing gave her every reason to be neurotic, is explained thus:

> Born of a delicate and overworked mother, and an impulsive, hard, imaginative father, who did not look with favor upon her coming into the world, Louise was from childhood a neurotic, one of the race of oversensitive women that in later days industrialism was to bring in such great numbers into the world.

Yet if anything emerges from the story of Louise and
of other Winesburg characters it is that their neuroses
and frustrations are the consequence of the drab, repressed
life in a small town before the coming of the Model T
Ford gave them a little freedom.

In *Poor White* Anderson made a muddled attempt
to find human values in the new industrial world. Hugh
McVey, the son of a Pap Finn type, allows the motherly
wife of a station agent to civilize him, but in so doing
he loses his humanity, symbolized by his tendency to
dream. Eventually he becomes the inventor and manufacturer of a plant-setting machine. When he marries
Clara, he is so dehumanized that he cannot establish a
vital relationship. The climax comes when the crazed old
harness maker, Joe Wainworth, kills his employee, Jim
Gibson, who had ordered machine-made harnesses. Joe
slashes the harness to bits and then attacks Hugh. Clara,
riding with Hugh and her father in the latter's new car,
had been hating both men for their talk of machines.

> And then the past rose up to strike. It struck with
> claws and teeth; and the claws and teeth sank into
> Hugh's flesh, into the flesh of the man whose seed was
> already alive within her.
> At that moment the woman who had been a thinker
> stopped thinking. Within her arose the mother, fierce
> and indomitable, strong with the strength of the roots
> of a tree. To her then and forever after Hugh was no
> hero, remaking the world, but a perplexed boy hurt
> by life. He never again escaped out of boyhood in her
> consciousness of him. With the strength of a tigress
> she tore the crazed harness maker away from
> Hugh. . . .
> For Clara the thing for which she had hungered had
> she thought happened.

However a germ of the "disease of thinking" which had upset the harness maker's mind had got into Hugh's blood. Somewhat later Hugh and Clara stand by a fence in the moonlight. "The disease of thinking was making Hugh useless for the work of his age."

This mishmash of bad writing and confused ideas was praised by Mencken. It is, of course, an example of the neo-primitivism which infected the era. It has its ancestry in the call-of-the-wild writings of Jack London and its more sophisticated version in the blood-and-guts stories of Hemingway. One manifestation of this cult was the interest in the Negro—not the new Negro emerging from the cotton field and the ghetto, but the Negro as exemplar of the id not shackled by a machine civilization. The theme appears in Van Vechten's *Nigger Heaven* and Anderson's *Dark Laughter*. It showed itself in the enthusiasm of the intellectuals for New Orleans jazz. Vachel Lindsay, hearing it,

. . . SAW THE CONGO, CREEPING THROUGH THE BLACK, CUTTING THROUGH THE JUNGLE WITH A GOLDEN TRACK

Lindsay, of course, did not approve: Negroes were to be redeemed by means of an almost equally primitive evangelical religion on the order of General William Booth's. It was the other side of the same coin.

On a less Freudian level the crusade against the machine took on Wordsworthian coloring with the glorification of the man close to the soil. Here poetry and politics got confused as they did in the Romantic movement. The noble peasant was a feature of the landscape as in Gray's *Elegy* and Wordsworth's *Leech Gatherer*, but he was also a better man than the lord who exploited him as in the poetry of Goldsmith and Burns. So too in American literature the Populist economic and political struggle against the exploitation of the farmer developed the Romantic myth of the yokel as morally and aesthetically finer than the city man.*

The myth was not invented during the second renaissance; in America it is at least as old as Whittier's *Barefoot Boy*. But the writers of what should have been a more sophisticated period preserved it long after the barefoot boy had become an anachronism. The physical and intelligence tests of World War I showed that years of migration by the talented to the city and the poorer educational opportunities outside of an urban-industrial environment had stunted both the minds and the bodies of the country boys.

Nevertheless Willa Cather could write in *The Song of the Lark* (1915)

> The rich city, fat with food and drink, is a spent thing; its chief concern is with its digestion and its little game of hide-and-seek with the undertaker.

Somewhat inconsistently she represented the small-town Dr. Archie in a New York restaurant as thinking that the people around him look happier than those in his native West.

Her mixture of populism and machine phobia comes out in *One of Ours* (1922). As Lewis had done in *Main Street,* she pictured the farmer as doing useful work;

* It was a myth which helped preserve the rural domination of state legislatures until the one-man-one-vote decision of the Supreme Court in 1963.

whereas the village and the city are parasitical. She contrasted the useful things produced by the farmer; corn, wheat, hogs, with what he bought: "manufactured articles of poor quality. . . . Most of his money was paid out for machinery and that too went to pieces. A steam thresher didn't last long; a horse outlived three automobiles." She did not mention that before the advent of science and labor-saving machinery a farmer often outlived three wives.

In that novel young Claude meets the Erlicks who live without machines:

> They merely knew how to live, he discovered, and spent their money on themselves, instead of on machines to do the work and machines to entertain people. Machines, Claude decided, could not make pleasure, whatever else they could do.*

There is a characteristic vagueness here: the word *machines* is somehow menacing. What machines did they did not spend money on—an automobile or a phonograph, a washing machine or a vacuum cleaner? Did she consider a handcrafted privy more aesthetic than a machine-made indoor toilet? And who did the cleaning and the wash? People like the Erlicks, who had leisure for talk, must have had access to cheap domestic help.

Like Sinclair Lewis, Miss Cather had a valid case against the narrow commercialism of many Americans. But like Edgar Lee Masters and Sherwood Anderson she tended to romanticize a pre-industrial past and the people of more primitive cultures. Thus in a modern village:

* In *Godey's Lady's Book* the editor, Sarah Josepha Hale, campaigned for washing machines and sewing machines to ease women's drudgery. Isabelle Webb Entrikin, *Sarah Josepha Hale* and *Godey's Lady's Book*, Philadelphia, 1946, p. 109.

The people themselves had changed. He could remember when all the farmers in the community were friendly toward each other; now they were continually having lawsuits.* Their sons were either stingy, or extravagant or lazy.

The picture in 1922 is very similar to James Fenimore's view of Americans a hundred years before: for him too the mythical good old virtues had gone.

However people of more primitive cultures might still be admirable. Thus in *The Song of the Lark,* Thea goes to a Mexican dance. There, unlike those of her village, the men are courteous to the women and do not indulge in the horseplay of bumping into other couples. "Thea could not help wondering whether the Mexicans had no jealousies or neighborly grudges as the people of Moonstone had." It apparently did not occur to her that a collision on the dance floor or a discourteous remark might lead to a knife in the ribs. Cather never mentions the Mexican habit of turning a fete into a drunken revel.

Thea was entirely right in preferring to sing with the Mexicans rather than in the dreary choir of her father's church. In 1915 it was valid social criticism to point up the artistic shortcomings of America—a heritage less of the industrial revolution than of the combination of the legacies of British culture and the cutting of roots involved in the western migration. The Puritan revolution had silenced England as "a nest of singing birds," and there was no room for a piano on the covered wagon. In long-settled rural communities the old ballads survived; in metro-

---

* A prominent professor of law thinks that with the stabilization of boundary lines there was probably a decline in lawsuits. Certainly the proportion of lawyers and judges in the population declined from 1 for every 704 persons in 1900 to 1 in 875 for 1920.

politan areas there were orchestras and operas. But except among such groups as those of Welsh, Italian, or German extraction, folk music of high quality was not a part of the American heritage. The player piano and the phonograph did not kill a native artistry; if anything they sewed the seeds of a musical renaissance.

Like so many writers of her period Willa Cather propagated doctrines that became clichés among the intellectuals: that philistinism was peculiarly American; that people of earlier periods or other cultures were superior to contemporary Americans; that rural folk were aesthetically and morally finer than city people; and that commerce and industry were entirely baleful forces. In a story written in 1930 and published two years later she combined a number of these themes. Neighbor Rosicky, from whom the story takes its name, is a Czech farmer in the midwest. Unlike his American neighbors he and his wife are content "not to hurry through life, not be always skimping and saving." The children of their neighbors as described by Mary were, "Pale pinched little things, they look like skimmed milk. I'd rather put some colour into my children's faces than put money in the bank." Because his son's American wife is a town girl, Rosicky worries that she will be discontented with farm life. So one Saturday he takes the Ford over to his son's house and tells him to take Polly to the movies while he, Rosicky, does the dishes—an act not especially characteristic of European born men. As he scours the pots and pans, he meditates that "Generally speaking, marrying an American girl was certainly a risk. . . ."

> He was afraid Polly would grow so discontented that Rudy would quit the farm and take a factory job in Omaha . . . to Rosicky that meant the end of every-

thing for his son. To be a landless man was to be a wage-earner, a slave, all your life, to have nothing, to be nothing.

Rosicky himself was originally a city man; he had been a tailor in London and New York, but

> In the country, if you had a mean neighbor, you could keep off his land and make him keep off yours.* But in the city, all the foulness and misery and brutality of your neighbors was part of your life. . . . There were mean people everywhere, to be sure, even in their own country town here. But they weren't tempered, hardened, sharpened, like the treacherous people in cities who live by grinding or cheating or poisoning their fellow men.

Rosicky is the populist stereotype of the farmer; kindly and generous, a loving husband and father, a man contented with a bare living got by hard work. In the story he is so completely without fault that he is more unreal than Wordsworth's noble yokels. And the evil city man might do as a stage villain. Hamlin Garland had portrayed Stephen Council as such a farmer in his story *Under the Lion's Paw* (1891). But Garland, who had worked on a farm, did not glamorize the life. The man whom Council helps to get started has to drive himself, his wife, and his boy to labor from early morning until well into the night.

> No slave in the Roman galleys could have toiled so frightfully and lived, for this man thought himself a free man, and that he was working for his wife and babes.

---

* A well-known rural method was to use a shot-gun loaded with rock salt.

As for the happy life of the farm boy:

> An infinitely pathetic but common figure—this boy
> on the American farm, where there is no law against
> child labor. To see him in his coarse clothing, his huge
> boots, and his ragged cap, as he staggered with a pail
> of water from the well, or trudged in the cold and
> cheerless dawn into the frosty field behind his team,
> gave the city-bred visitor a sharp pang of sympathetic
> pain.

But Garland's was the voice of an earlier generation;
Willa Cather's of the second renaissance, when it became
fashionable to picture people without technology as happier than those with it. Thus Waldo Frank in *Rediscovery
of America* (1929) could write:

> There is more famine in the Sahara, but more com-
> fort. There is more misery in Poland, in Egypt, and
> more comfort. All western Europe, despite primitive
> farms, decadent towns, and the growing gnaw of dynas-
> tic discord, is vastly superior in common comfort to
> our comfort-worshiping Republic.
> . . . in cultured worlds like China, India, France
> man achieved insight within himself and into his rela-
> tion with the whole of life, which gave him wisdom to
> equilibrate the forces that beset him.[7]

No evidence is cited, and just how famine and misery are
consistent with comfort would make sense only to someone
dealing with intellectual abstractions.

Intellectuals, like herring, tend to move in schools.
Thus despite all the noisy quarrels of the period it is
obvious that those on both the left and the right, the new

humanists and their enemies, a realist like Dreiser and a romantic like Cabell, a caricaturist like Lewis and a symbolist like Eliot all agreed that American culture was in a parlous state. With varying emphasis they blamed technology and the machine. The left-wing emphasized capitalist greed; the right wing talked about the destruction of spiritual values. All tended to find that man had been better off in some earlier or foreign culture. Pound's Provence; Eliot's composite world of Dante and Spenser; the pre-industrial world of Masters, Anderson and Cather; Mencken's Munich or his aristocratic South; Frank's India or China; Mumford's Concord; Hemingway's Spain were all beautiful isles of somewhere compared to twentieth-century America.

But the most fully exploited never-never land was the Old South as seen through the eyes of the self-styled Agrarians. This group of poets and professors, originally centered at Vanderbilt University in Nashville, began their association with the publication of a fine magazine of poetry, symbolically called *The Fugitive* (1922–1925). Beginning with John Crowe Ransom's essay "The South— Old and New" in *The Sewanee Review* for April 1925 they turned to social criticism. The Agrarian movement was in part triggered by the Scopes trial at Dayton. At Vanderbilt University Professor Edwin Mims suggested to the men who had produced *The Fugitive* that they write letters and essays to show that the South was not like the caricature drawn by Mencken and Pegler during the trial.[8]

Ironically the idealized portrait of the Old South drawn by Ransom and his associates was strikingly like the one Mencken had sketched—a land flowing with culture and gracious living. Thus in Ransom's view the farmer had been able "to envelop his work and his play with a leisure which permitted the maximum activity of intelligence." [9] In the manifesto, *I'll Take My Stand* (1930) Ransom and Allen Tate argued that an industrial society would extinguish the meaning of the arts as humanity had known them in the past. They held that the arts had flourished under an agrarian dispensation. As John L. Stewart remarks in his study of the Agrarians ". . . when one reads [in Donald Davidson's essay] that only in an agrarian society does there remain much of a balanced life, where the arts are not luxuries to be purchased but belong *as a matter of course* in the routine of his living, one begins to pull back, especially when one is told that this happy balance obtained in the Old South." [10] Davidson went on to say that the South had always practiced the more sophisticated arts as a matter of course.*

As we have seen, large generalizations are characteristic of the social criticism of the period. When he came to specifics about the arts Davidson listed Chivers, Kennedy, Byrd, Longstreet, Sut Levengood, Cooke, Page, Cable, and Allen. It is worth noting that Cable, the one important writer in this roster, treated Southern themes, as in *The Silent South,* a book on the Negro problem, in a way that proved offensive to his native region, and that he settled permanently in Northampton, Massachusetts. Before the Civil War one of the few Southern painters of any note, Washington Allston, after a stay in England, settled in Cambridge, Massachusetts; Poe fled Richmond for Philadelphia.

* Cf. W. J. Cash: "In general, the intellectual and aesthetic culture of the Old South was a superficial and jejune thing, borrowed from without and worn as a political armor and a badge of rank; . . ." Wilbur J. Cash, *The Mind of the South,* N. Y., 1939, p. 94.

As has been suggested, distaste for industrialism was colored by a preference for the pillared portico. Thus Allen Tate could write:

> The institution of slavery was a positive good only in the sense that Calhoun had argued that it was: it had become a necessary element in a stable society. He had argued justly that only in a society of fixed classes can men be free. Only men who are socially as well as economically secure can preserve the historical sense of obligation. This historical sense of obligation implied a certain freedom to do right.[11]

Tate conveniently forgot that Jefferson had pointed out that it was precisely this freedom to do right which was destroyed by slavery:

> . . . man is an imitative animal. This quality is the germ of all education in him. From his cradle to his grave he is learning to do what he sees others do. If a parent could find no motive either in his philosophy or his self-love for restraining the intemperance of passion towards his slave, it should always be a sufficient one that his child is present. But generally it is not sufficient. The parent storms, the child looks on, catches the lineaments of wrath, puts on the same airs in the circle of smaller slaves, gives loose to his worst of passions, and thus nursed, educated and daily exercised in tyranny, cannot but be stamped by it with odious peculiarities.* [12]

* Such accounts of the ante-bellum South as that of Frances Kemble show how laws, customs, and economics gave little freedom for even a humane slave-holder to do right.

Yet somehow or other the Agrarians combined a defense of slavery with idyllic pictures of the life of the independent farmer, who in actuality, under the plantation system, had often been relegated to marginal land and subsistence living.

The old-time religion got into the picture. In *God Without Thunder* (1930) Ransom, like Irving Babbitt, rewrote the Bible to suit his predilections:

> As I understand the myth of the Garden of Eden, it meant to express something substantially like this: Satan is the Demigod, the Prometheus, *the Spirit of Secular Science* [Ital. mine], who would like to set up falsely as God, the Ruler of the Universe—beware of him.[13]

Arguing that Christ did not claim to be part of the Godhead, Ransom stated:

> Industrialism is the effect of a Christianity that has elevated the Man-God to the throne of Jehovah and made of Christ the temporal Messiah that he intended not to be.[14]

This of course ignores the fact that the worship of Christ as part of the Godhead especially flourishes in agricultural societies.

Ransom then argued that farmers as contrasted with industrialists were truly religious; "they find God a reality when they make contact with the soil." [15] Ransom did not mention that during the twenties the most characteristic expression of this religion was the Ku Klux Klan. For him:

To turn away—to turn forward, as the progressives always have it—from this idyllic simplicity of life is to seek to improve the human position at the expense of nature as an enemy, to eat of the fruit of the tree of knowledge, to break the man-to-God relation, and to commit sin.[16]

As is usual in so much of the technophobic discussion the enemy was personified by capitals:

Work, Power, Activity, Business, Industry, Production—these are the great words of an age of applied science. They do beautifully for those who need them badly enough and are willing to abandon their deepest personal interests. . . . They are deeply Occidental, and they are quite scorned by Orientals, who insist upon their contemplation and their inner development. . . .[17]

There is of course no recognition that in the meantime millions of Orientals were starving, to be later fed by American Production. In fact Ransom went so far as to attack the humanitarian efforts of the biological and social sciences:

The products of these sciences are not too welcome to the person with aesthetic gifts . . . they submerge his sensibility in their intensely practical and exclusive process. Life seems to lose its dignity if it has to be lived with so much fuss.[18]

One may be permitted to wonder how much dignity there was in the lives of people plagued by malaria and hookworm. Before the discoveries of biological sciences those diseases did however contribute greatly to the Southern farmer's lassitude, not quite the leisure so much praised by the Agrarians.

As opposed to this Eden, "Industrialism assumes that man is merely a creature of instincts [that] his life consists entirely in the satisfaction of his appetites." There are no Jeeter Lesters or Tobacco Roads in the South of Ransom, Tate, and Davidson.

One can grant that industrialism brought evils: slums, coal towns, sweated labor, and spoiled landscape. The Progressives before World War I had recognized these and addressed themselves to their amelioration and possible cure.

On the other hand much of the romantic crusade against technology was specious: it failed to recognize that an America of 122,000,000 people in 1930 could not be adequately housed, clothed, and fed without the machine; they harked back to an idyllic past which had existed for only a fraction of the population, and which for even that fraction was far less idyllic than the nostalgic fantasy. These crusaders dealt less with facts than with verbal symbols. They were fond of pejorative and question-begging terms. Take Ransom's "satisfaction of appetites": the implication is sensuality, but what industrialism produced was first of all food, fuel, clothing and shelter, plus the means of storing and transporting these goods. Even a farmer, if he lived in the prairie states, had to get lumber and fuel from a distance. As this discussion has shown, these writers dealt in abstractions and personifications. Like Milton's Hell their America was peopled by demons; only instead of Mammon there was Business; instead of Moloch there was Industry or the Machine; instead of Beelzebub there was Science or Technology.

Milton, like Blake at a later period, was representing elements in man's psyche like greed or cruelty; the romantic crusaders adopted the pathetic fallacy—they gave human qualities to the machine or to industrialism. What is worse, by creating a demonology they destroyed much of their value as social critics. Science and technology and the resulting business and industrial complex did need critical examination—desperately so, as events proved after 1929. But having translated these forces into malevolent abstractions the romantic crusaders failed to give any sort of balanced evaluation of science and technology. Instead they took the extreme position that these developments met no human need, that they were merely the result of greed and avarice—or to use Ransom's vocabulary—of Sin.

The mystique of the machine as an evil force appears in O'Neill's *Dynamo* (1929) in which a young man, Ruben Light, comes to worship the dynamo as the great mother:

O Dynamo, who gives life to things, hear my prayer! Grant me the miracle of your love!

When a girl offers him human love, Ruben calls her a harlot and shoots her:

Mother [the Dynamo] . . . I did it for your sake!

As Anna Russell remarked after retelling one of Wagner's plots, "I'm not making this up."

It is not too much to say that during the period under discussion the poets, novelists, playwrights, and literary critics were almost universally hostile to science and technology. As the foregoing discussion suggests, this hostility was an uncritical, emotional response which manifested itself in generalizations and abstractions. For any genuinely critical evaluation of science and technology we must look to cultural historians like Thorstein Veblen or Lewis Mumford.

Thus Veblen cited statistics which showed that city people had a shorter life expectancy than those in rural areas. In *The Instinct of Workmanship* (1914) he traced the development of technology, a development long antedating the Industrial Revolution which began in the latter part of the eighteenth century. The beginning of the machine industry, he said, developed out of handicraft technology, "particularly at conjunctures where that technology is called on to deal with such large mechanical problems as exceed the force of manual labour or that elude the reach of the craftsman's tools." [19] Nor was routine exclusively a product of the machine: for instance "the punctilios of religious observance may come to be a very rigid routine." [20]

On the other hand such beneficent inventions as the telephone, the typewriter, and the automobile "may have wasted more effort and substance than they have saved." [21] By a kind of Parkinson's Law they generated an increase in the volume of traffic per unit of outcome.

Whether or not one agrees with Veblen, it is obvious that, unlike the literary fraternity, he was discussing technology in an informed and judicial manner. Here are no abstract monsters, no capitalized personifications; Veblen discussed clocks, cultivators, scientific stock breeding, telephones, and motor cars. He pointed out that the growing complexity of the machine age made it necessary to educate more and more of the population. He dealt with the questions of social control of the industrial system and of a monopoly of its surplus by owners and managers.

In much greater detail than Veblen, Lewis Mumford traced the complex history of technology. Like Veblen he attempted an assessment of the impact of technology on society. Although *Technics and Civilization* was published in 1934 Mumford said that the first draft of the book was written in 1930. Obviously, with its mass of scholarly detail, it had been long in preparation. Not unfairly then it may be taken as representing certain aspects of the sensibility of the 1920s. Mumford has been variously a professor of the humanities, a historian of architecture and technology, an expert on town planning, and a social critic. It would be impossible in a short space to analyze and evaluate his achievement as a whole. But even a cursory examination of *Technics and Civilization* will show that Mumford's attempt at a critical examination is seriously flawed because of his acceptance of a number of the intellectual clichés of the 1920s.

One of these clichés was that mechanization was forced upon society by capitalist greed:

> . . . under capitalist direction the aim of mechaniza-
> tion is not to save labor but to eliminate all labor
> except that which can be channeled at a profit through
> the factory.[22]

This vast oversimplification with its personification—here without capitals—of mechanization is obviously a reflection of the *zeitgeist* discussed in this chapter. The fact is that some of the most remarkable results of mechanization appeared not in the factory but on the farm. When in 1793 Jefferson imported a threshing machine, a man with a flail could thresh only 7 bushels of wheat a day. With the new machine six men could do 150 bushels—an average of 25 per man. The machine saved money, of course, but it released men and women from the monotonous labor of wielding a flail. With a sickle, common in Europe and still used in Colonial America, a man by means of back-breaking labor, could harvest half an acre a day. In 1852 two men with a McCormick reaper could do 10 or 12 times that much.[23] Between 1800 and 1900 the man-hours required to harvest and thresh an acre of wheat were reduced from 40 to 8.[24] Wordsworth's solitary reaper and Keats' girl on the granary floor were more appealing to the poets than to the farmer.

It is even doubtful that every village mechanic trying to build an automobile was chiefly interested in channeling his invention through a factory for profit. Like the true scientist, the dedicated inventor is usually interested in proving that his theories are valid—that the thing will work. The Stanley twins were notorious for their refusal to adopt mass production of their fearful and wonderful steam car. Like many other early inventors of motor cars the Stanleys were what a later generation would call hot-rodders—a dedicated brotherhood which will waste money and risk life to achieve mechanical superiority and sport. For instance, T. E. Stanley killed himself while speeding just for the fun of it. The aim of Orville and Wilbur Wright was certainly not primarily factories and profits; like Daedalus they wanted to be the first to achieve heavier than air flight. The search for profits came later.

Of course many inventors, like Samuel F. B. Morse and Henry Ford, were greedy for money. So too are some novelists and scientists. But the contention that machines are developed only to make money is no more sensible than Dr. Johnson's statement that no one but a blockhead ever wrote for any reason but money. Very often the machine, like the novel, poem, or scientific discovery, is the result of the human urge to create something new. Perhaps more often it was designed as a means of escape from stultifying routine labor. Hand sawn planks may delight the antique collector, but the working man preferred the steam-driven saw.

In pursuit of the argument that machine-capitalism has foisted unneeded goods upon the public Mumford wrote:

> Vacuum pumps driven by electric motors are *forced into American households* [ital. mine] for the purpose of cleaning an obsolete form of floor covering, the carpet or rug, whose appropriateness for use in interiors, if it did not disappear with the caravans where it originated, passed out of existence with rubber heels and steam-heated houses.[25]

Apparently Mumford's ideal interior would resemble a hospital room.

This kind of doctrinaire approach appears in his remarks about the telephone:

> One of the blessings of invention, among the naive advocates of the machine, is that it does away with the need for imagination; instead of holding a conversation with one's dearest friend in reverie, one may pick up a telephone and substitute his voice for one's fantasy.[26]

It apparently did not occur to him that the parents of overdue teen-agers can have some highly unpleasant fantasies until a welcome voice on the telephone dispels them, or that lonely old people have more than their fill of reverie and imaginary conversations.

Mumford even deplored the pasteurization of milk on the ground that it was a makeshift made necessary by the distance between the cow and the consumer. If we would only redistribute the population nearer rural centers "the elaborate mechanical apparatus for counteracting distances and space may to a degree be diminished." The mechanical apparatus used in pasteurization did nothing to improve the product, it merely robbed the milk of some of its value as nutriment. He seems to have been unaware of the fact that raw milk direct from the cow may carry the germs of tuberculosis and undulant fever.

After citing pasteurization as a typical mechanical perversion he went on:

> One might multiply such examples from many departments: they point to a fact about the machine that has not been generally recognized by those quaint apologists for machine-capitalism who look upon every extra expenditure of horsepower and every fresh piece of mechanical apparatus as an automatic net gain in efficiency.[27]

One might just as easily use the *et tu* answer: "Those quaint apologists for the natural life look upon every machine as an automatic enemy."

And of course by reiterating the phrase *machine-capitalism* the writer evokes the Marxist bogeyman. Sure enough we come upon other Marxist stereotypes: ". . . the ruling classes and their imitators among the lesser bourgoisie." The terms are in themselves pejorative and they grossly oversimplify the American social structure. In any case these refugees from the factory and the office retreated into "a fake non-mechanical environment. . . ."

> This private world, as lived in Suburbia or in the more palatial country houses, is not to be differentiated by any objective standard from the world in which the lunatic attempts to live out the drama in which he appears to himself . . . to be Lorenzo the Magnificent or Louis XIV.
> . . . indeed, the additions of 'comforts' made them padded cells.[28]

One could ask the famous question, "Who's looney now?" This is the language not of social criticism but of paranoia. If the evidence presented in this chapter suggests anything, it is that the writers of the second renaissance when they considered machine technology did become paranoid. All of them of necessity utilized the products of science and technology. Few if any of them refused to use the railroad, the motor car, the bathroom, the telephone, much as they might deplore THE MACHINE. Their diatribes were prepared on a typewriter, set by a linotype, and printed by a rotary press. It is not recorded that any of them built a hut on Walden Pond. Almost none of their discussion had the basic sanity of Emerson's Ode to Channing:

> There are two laws discrete,
> Not reconciled,—
> Law for man, and law for thing;
> The last builds town and fleet,
> But it runs wild,
> And doth the man unking.

'Tis fit the forest fall,
The steep be graded,
The mountain tunnelled,
The sand shaded,
The orchard planted,
The glebe tilled,
The prairie granted,
The steamer built.

Let man serve law for man:
Live for friendship, live for love
For truth's sake and harmony's behoof;
The state may follow how it can
As Olympus follows Jove.

Like the intellectuals of the second renaissance Emerson believed that:

Things are in the saddle
And ride mankind.

But he recognized that things could include not only the railroad and the steamship but the orchard and the glebe. Thoreau compared the ownership of a farm to a sentence in the county jail. For Emerson "things" were not evils to be banished; rather they were instrumentalities to be used for necessary purposes. The problem was to keep the two laws discrete—to keep humane ends in view.

The writers under discussion also had the admirable purpose of defining and furthering humane ends. But fanaticism even for human values is of necessity inhumane. The fanatic sees the world in terms of absolutes of good and evil: agriculture versus industry; idealized farmer versus factory slave; worker versus capitalist; Man versus

Machine. In all ages the fanatic whether religious, Marxist, or Birchite is given to paranoid distortion of reality. If the foregoing discussion is not in itself a distortion, it demonstrates that the intellectuals of the second American renaissance displayed a considerable amount of fanaticism in their attack on science and technology.

7.

The Paranoid Picture

One of the chief characteristics of the paranoid is that he feels menaced by hostile persons or forces. He is unable to distinguish between real and imaginary dangers. As has been implied in the foregoing discussion there was a paranoid quality in the literature about Puritanism, capitalism, democracy, and technology. Of course, a social critic who points out the flaws in the existing order is not necessarily paranoid; he becomes so only when he magnifies minor discomforts into overpowering menaces.

The difference between social criticism and paranoia is often revealed in apocalyptic statements such as have been quoted throughout this study. Too often the intellectuals have resembled Franklin's ephemera who thought that the setting sun meant the end of the world. Like the white-robed fanatics so beloved by cartoonists, the paranoiac has a penchant for carrying signs saying, "Prepare to meet thy doom!" Thus in *The Hollow Men* Eliot prophesied that the world would end "not with a bang but a whimper"—which of course now seems the more unlikely of the two alternatives.

There is more than a little paranoia in the only-in-America theme that runs through so much of the writing of the period. It was the dominant note of *Civilization in the United States, An Inquiry by Thirty Americans* (1922) edited by Harold Stearns—a book sometimes nicknamed *The Thirty Against America*. (Alfred Kazin called it a "famous inquest over American culture.")[1] The writers were on the whole a distinguished group, including H. L. Mencken, Lewis Mumford, Robert Morss Lovett, Van Wyck Brooks, George Jean Nathan, H. W. Van Loon, Katherine Anthony, John Macy, and Joel Spingarn. Harold Stearns' comment is typical:

> To an extent almost incomprehensible to the peoples of older cultures, the things of the mind and spirit have been given over, in America, into the almost exclusive custody of women. . . .[2]
>
> Our intellectual life, when we judge it objectively on the side of vigour and diversity, too often seems to be a democracy of mountebanks.[3]

John Macy asserted that "yellow journalism has swamped the whole press";[4] Joel Spingarn said that "America has no scholarship because as yet it has a body but no soul."[5] As James Boyd summed it up in the chapter, "As an Irishman Sees It":

> It is now rare to find a young American who does not cry out against American civilization.[6]

It is significant that the two most widely hailed books of poetry in the first quarter of this century both pictured modern society as a kind of wasteland. In fact the title of one of them has become a descriptive cliché. In view of the towering reputation of T. S. Eliot it may seem strange today to mention in the same breath Edgar Lee Masters whose repute has largely faded. But in 1915 Ezra Pound, congratulating Harriet Monroe on the publication of *Prufrock,* wrote that among contemporary poets Eliot and Masters "are the best of the bilin [sic]." [7] Writing in *The Seven Arts* for 1917 Theodore Dreiser said that since Whitman, America had produced one poet, Edgar Lee Masters.[8] Van Wyck Brooks in 1918 spoke of the book's "immense and legitimate vogue." [9] And Sinclair Lewis in his Nobel Prize speech of 1930 praised it as being "utterly different from any other poetry ever published."

Today the reportorial, often flat statements in *Spoon River* seem naive in an era nurtured on Eliot. Masters' rhythms lack the polish and intricacies we have learned to appreciate. His structure has much of the do-it-yourself architecture of a midwestern balloon-framed house; Eliot's has the borrowed luxury of Mrs. Jack Gardner's Fenway Court.

But in some ways *Spoon River* and *The Waste Land* have odd similarities—the most important being that each represents modern society as dismal and arid. By means of a series of vignettes both present a panoramic view of that society. Both Eliot and Masters contrast an allegedly more vital past with an enervated present. Thus Lucinda Matlock (a character based on Masters' grandmother) after telling of her vigorous, happy life of ninety-six years, addressed the present generation as

Degenerate sons and daughters
Life is too strong for you—
It takes life to love Life.

The photographer, Rutherford McDowell, contrasting the faces of the pioneers in the old ambrotypes with those of the present:

Freely did my camera record their faces too,
With so much of the old strength gone,
And the old faith gone,
And the mastery of life gone,
And the old courage gone
Which labors and loves and suffers and sings
Under the sun!

It is the sort of contrast which Eliot gives in a very different way between Cleopatra in her barge and the bored modern woman in the luxurious boudoir; between Spenser's nymphs gathering flowers along the Thames and the modern nymphs who leave empty bottles, sandwich papers, silk handkerchiefs, cardboard boxes, cigarette ends and "other testimony of summer nights."

Both poets can be accused of glamorizing a somewhat mythical past at the expense of the present. In Spenser's England there were certainly counterparts to the modern untidy nymphs; witness Shakespeare's Audrey, Mistress Quickly, and Doll Tearsheet. Elizabethan memoirs suggest that ladies-in-waiting were a rather more earthy breed than the idealized nymphs of Spenser's poem. And among the women that Masters knew were Jane Addams and Willa Cather—women as admirable as the rural Lucinda Matlock of an earlier generation. It is as if Eliot based his social criticism on a comparison of paintings by Watteau and George Bellows; as if Masters compared a Daniel Chester French statute in the park with the people sprawled there.

Leaving aside a consideration of the artistic merits of *The Waste Land,* one can find justification for Bernard De Voto's contention that it misrepresented the common people. During the blitz the dismal Cockney women in the pub, the young man carbuncular, the untidy typist rose to heights of heroism that would have done credit to the men of Thermopolae.

It may seem unfair to suggest that Eliot should have foreseen the heroism of the British in World War II, but is it? After all, the undersized, underfed Cockney of World War I had marched off to death gaily singing "It's a long way to Tipperary" and "Pack up your troubles in your old kit bag." Pound had seen this quality:

> fortitude as never before
> frankness as never before
> disillusions as never told in the old days, . . .

> There died a myriad
> And of the best, among them
> For an old bitch gone in the teeth,
> For a botched civilization,

There was justice in Pound's "botched civilization" but it was not the common man who had botched it. World War I was the product of an essentially aristocratic society to which Eliot kowtowed.

If Eliot's picture of the wasteland of modern society had been merely a portrait of England of the 1920s it would not be especially pertinent to a discussion of the literary and social scene in the United States, but the poem was properly recognized as a critique of all modern life. Eliot himself said in 1959, "I'd say that my poetry has obviously more in common with my distinguished contemporaries in America than with anything written in England. In its emotional springs it comes from America." [10] It is possible to accept his earlier poems as valid portraits of ineffectual or defeated persons, but the obvious premise of *The Waste Land* is that all moderns are defeated as contrasted with the more vital people of the past. Thus it suggests the paranoid obsession of unique tribulation.

All this is not intended to suggest that *The Waste Land* is not a great work of art. Eliot and his followers insisted that a poem should be considered only as a work of art. However literature, unlike its sister arts, deals with ideas and it is with ideas that the present study is chiefly concerned. Judged by that criteria *The Waste Land* as a critique of society fails to reflect the vitality, admirable or not, of modern society; like the novels of Henry James it has a valetudinarian quality. How did Eliot know that the typist got no fun out of her affair with the house agent's clerk? The Shakepeherian Rag was originally a spoof and no doubt good to dance to. The modern "nymphs" along the Thames may have enjoyed themselves as much as Spenser's green-haired damsels, and in much the same way.

By the time he came to *East Coker* Eliot was writing such observations as

> The whole world is our hospital
> Endowed by the ruined millionaire . . .

With some justice Karl Shapiro charged that the "vulgarity of thought and its expression is hardly superior to 'Only

God can make a tree.' " [11] Indeed a number of pessimistic passages in the poem are not notable for originality of thought or expression—for instance:

> O dark dark dark. They all go into the dark,
> The vacant interstellar spaces, the vacant
>   into the vacant,
> The captains, merchant bankers, eminent
>   men of letters,
> The generous patrons of art, the statesmen
>   and the rulers,
> Distinguished civil servants, chairmen of
>   many committees,
> Industrial lords and petty contractors, all
>   go into the dark . . .

On this theme Masters was rather more poetic and was closer to the ancient tradition of the *ubi sunt* theme:

> Where are Elmer, Herman, Bert, Tom and Charley
> The weak of will, the strong of arm, the clown, the
>   boozer, the fighter?
> All, all are sleeping on the hill . . .

> Where are Uncle Isaac and Aunt Emily,
> And old Towny Kincaid and Sevigne Houghton,
> And Major Walker who had talked
> With venerable men of the revolution?—
> All, all, are sleeping on the hill . . .

> Where is Old Fiddler Jones
> Who played with life all his ninety years,
> Braving the sleet with bared breast,
> Drinking, rioting, thinking neither of wife nor kin,
> Nor gold, nor love, nor heaven?

Lo! he babbles of the fish-frys of long ago,
Of the horse-races of long ago at Clary's Grove,
Of what Abe Lincoln said
One time at Springfield.

This is the difference between the poetry of life and that of the library. Masters' Fiddler Jones is a person; Eliot's Sweeney is a personification like his typist; his captains, merchant bankers, statesmen, and rulers are as much abstractions as are the proletariat and the bourgeoisie of the leftist writers. It was Blake, a lower class poet whom Eliot wrote of with a certain superciliousness, who defined this habit of mind; "To generalize is to be an idiot."

The difference between the Eliot and Masters is not merely one of literary strategy. Masters, like Dreiser, Sherwood Anderson, and Sinclair Lewis, drawing their material from first-hand experience, showed people as enjoying and suffering human beings; Eliot watching them from the window saw them as the crowd which flowed up King William Street. Eliot's view is that of the typical intellectual who views society with distaste rather than compassion.

Thus Masters' *Spoon River,* dismal as it is in some respects, is by no means a scene of unrelieved gloom. There are fulfilled women as well as frustrated women, men of courage as well as cowards, saintly characters as well as sinners. Unlike Eliot who in *Ash Wednesday* had to "construct something/Upon which to rejoice, " Masters' poems are filled with the Jeffersonian ideal of free inquiry, humanitarianism and social justice. The names which echo through the minds of the characters are Jefferson, Lincoln, Atgeld, and Bryan; there are memories of the heroism at Valley Forge, Starved Rock, Missionary Ridge, and the war in the Philippines.

Spoon River is indeed an indictment of certain aspects of American civilization: Puritanism, materialism, narrow religion, and hypocrisy. But at times it echoes Lear's cry against the gods. The scientist Schofield Huxley, after telling of man's achievements, asks of God:

> How would you like to create a sun
> And the next day have worms
> Slipping in and out between your fingers?

However, along with this tragic view of life there is the transcendental note of hope. Thus Alfonso Churchill, who taught astronomy at Knox College,

> . . . preached the greatness of man,
> Who is none the less a part of the scheme of things
> For the distance of Spica or the Spiral Nebulae;
> Nor any the less part of the question
> Of what the drama means.

The Village Atheist after reading the *Upanishads* experiences a sense of revelation:

> Listen to me, ye who live in the senses
> And think through the senses only:
> Immortality is not a gift,
> Immortality is an achievement;
> And only those who strive mightily
> Shall possess it.

Unfortunately for his later reputation Masters did not render this in Sanskrit.

By contrast Eliot's finer artistic creation is essentially paranoid in its unrelieved gloom. But as Pound said,

> The age demanded an image
> Of its accelerated grimace . . .

Until the appearance of *The Waste Land, The Spoon River Anthology* was seized upon as giving that image. Its transcendental and idealistic elements were largely ignored. As late as 1962 May Swenson, editor of the paperback edition, wrote, "He had torn the veil of respectability from small-town life; Spoon River became the precursor of Sherwood Anderson's Winesburg and Sinclair Lewis' Gopher Prairie." That is less a summing up of *The Spoon River Anthology* than it is a description of what the critics thought the book to be about. It is small wonder that intellectuals nurtured on the early Van Wyck Brooks, on Waldo Frank and H. L. Mencken seized upon Eliot's far more pessimistic picture as their image of modern society.

The prose complement of *The Waste Land* was *The Modern Temper* by Joseph Wood Krutch. It became a leading document in the demonology of the era. In 1949 Frederic Hoffman wrote, "Of the hundreds of books and essays published in the 1920s on the matter of science and its gifts to man, two stand out as especially pertinent: Bertrand Russell's 'A Free Man's Worship' (1918) and Joseph Wood Krutch's *The Modern Temper* (1929)." [12] The description is somewhat inadequate: Krutch was concerned not merely with the impact of science but with the whole spectrum of modern thought. Science, which had robbed man of a belief in God, was also alleged to have reduced love to a biological function—a point Scott Fitzgerald never grasped. For Krutch modern literature dealt with littler people and less mighty emotions than did Sophocles or Shakespeare because "we have come, willy-nilly, to see the soul of man as commonplace and its emotions mean." Our cosmos lacks the dignity of tragedy: "The death of tragedy like the death of love, one of those emotional fatalities as a result of which the human as distinguished from the natural world *grows more and more a desert.*" [Ital. mine][13] Yet just a few years before this Woodrow Wilson had enacted a tragedy of Sophoclean or Shakespearean dimensions.

In this despairing mood Krutch saw Freudianism not as the basis for dealing with the ancient problem of mental illness but as "certainly the most far-reaching of any recent attempt to rob man of such shreds of dignity as has been left to him. . . ."[14] Disliking the ant-hill nature of Communist society Krutch nevertheless saw in the vitality of Russia, "the country of youthful barbarism," a possible hope for the future.

For the rest of us

> This world in which an unresolvable discord is the fundamental fact is the world in which we must continue to live, and for us wisdom must consist, not in searching for a means of escape which does not exist, but in making such peace with it as we may.[15]

In a conclusion worthy of *The Hollow Men* Krutch advised "the acceptance of such despair as must inevitably be ours" and quoted Milton's Satan:

> Hail horrors, hail
> Infernal world! and thou profoundest hell,
> Receive thy new possessor.

Obviously, if the contemporary world was incapable of tragedy, it could still manage melodrama.

This hand-clapped-to-the-brow attitude has already been remarked on in connection with Hemingway's "It's all a nothing" passages. It appears in Robinson Jeffers' *Shine, Perishing Republic* and his sentimentalizing of hawks: "I'd sooner, except the penalties, kill a man than a hawk. . . ." For him "Humanity is the mold to break away from, the atom to be split" and "the unsocial birds are a greater race." [16] Jeffers shared Hemingway's sentiment as reflected in the latter's remark that he was through serving time "for society, democracy and the other things." Thus Jeffers believed that the individual must "isolate himself morally to a certain extent or else degenerate too" [i.e., as America had].[17] Even more than Hemingway, Jeffers presented a world of unrelieved violence filled with murder, rape, incest, and putrefaction.

All this is of course true of Faulkner's world, but Faulkner was a better artist than Jeffers: he took in a more varied human scene. Furthermore Faulkner was writing about a region with a tragic history, a land, as he said, with a curse upon it. Granting all this, the Yoknapatawpha County as pictured in the early novels is a nightmare region. In *Sartoris* and *The Sound and the Fury* (both 1929) the old aristocracy like the Sartorises and the Compsons are decadent and self-destructive: the Sartoris men die through senseless recklessness ("Savages every one of 'em . . ." says Miss Jenny); Jason Compson III drinks himself to death; his son Quentin III, a student at Harvard, drowns himself because he is in love with his sister Candace, whom he knows to be a nymphomaniac; a brother, Maury, is a drooling idiot; Jason IV, who becomes head of the family, is almost a stage villain; he embezzles money Candace sends for the support of her daughter Quentin; he constantly threatens to beat the girl, who is seventeen; he burns some free tickets to a carnival rather than give them to a Negro servant who longs to attend. Quentin steals Jason's hidden $7000 and runs away with a carnival entertainer.

This theme of decay is present literally and symbolically in *As I Lay Dying* (1930), the story of a poor white family, The Bundrens, lugging the putrifying corpse of the mother back to her home town for burial. Cash, the best of the lot, breaks his leg and rides uncomplainingly for days on a springless wagon. Anse, the worthless father, and the insane Darl pour cement on Cash's leg, so that by the time they reach their destination grangrene has set in. Anse borrows some shovels from a woman living near the graveyard; then brings her home with him as his wife.

Here as elsewhere are incidents of gratuitous horror: the youngster Vardman boring holes in his mother's coffin and into her face; the boys listening to the bubbling of the corpse; the men tumbling the coffin end over end to get it away from the barn fire set by the insane Darl. And in *Sanctuary* (1931) there is the notorious incident of Popeye's violation of Temple Drake with a corncob. In that novel also there is an atmosphere of corruption: the young man, Gavin Stevens, is a compulsive drinker, and the flapper, Temple Drake, is thoroughly depraved.

Light in August (1932) tells the story of Joe Christmas, with a touch of Negro blood, who wantonly murders his Yankee mistress, sets her house on fire, then runs away, half willing himself to be caught. Joe is captured, killed, and castrated by Lieutenant Grimm, who thus compensates for his frustration at never having served in the World War. As Alfred Kazin has remarked, "There is always in Faulkner some final obsessive exaggeration. . . ." [18]

Kazin has also pointed out Faulkner's lack of a center: ". . . it has been possible to read into his work every point of view and prove them all." [19] Certainly his work shows a kind of love-hate relationship with the South. Like the Reverend Hightower of *Light in August* Faulkner hated slavery but dreamt of the Confederate past. Certainly there is a lot of Faulkner's view in Hightower's musing:

> Listening he seems to hear . . . the apotheosis of his own history, his own land, his own environed blood: that people . . . who can never take either pleasure or catastrophe or escape from either, without brawling over it. Pleasure, ecstasy, they cannot bear: their escape from it is violence, in drinking and fighting and praying; catastrophe too, the violence identical and apparently inescapable. *And so why should not their religion drive them to crucifixion of themselves and one another?*

At a later date in his Nobel Prize speech of 1950 Faulkner said:

> I decline to accept the end of man. . . . I believe that man will not merely endure; he will prevail . . . because he alone among creatures has a soul, a spirit capable of compassion and sacrifice and endurance. The poet's, the writer's duty is to write about these things. It is his privilege to help man endure by lifting his heart and reminding him of the courage and honor and hope and pride and compassion and pity and sacrifice which have been the glory of his past.[20]

Faulkner achieved some of this in the novelette, *The Bear,* but certainly his novels of the twenties and early thirties show little of this noble vision. Despite their tremendous vitality they present an almost unrelieved picture of decay, violence, and corruption. The occasional eloquent passages, the philosophical observations, resemble those lucid moments in a nightmare. Certainly a European reading Faulkner would conclude that the American South was a uniquely horrible place.

Faulkner's statement about the writer's duty and privilege "to help man endure by lifting his heart and reminding him of the courage and honor and hope and pride and compassion and sacrifice which have been the glory of his past" is a sad commentary on the work of the period, including his own. It was the evasion of this duty by so many of the writers of the second American renaissance which leads to the most serious indictment of their vision.

John Dos Passos is a case in point. For instance in *Three Soldiers* (1921) every sergeant, every commissioned officer without exception is pictured as a sadistic martinet. Before the men go to the front, an officer tells them that the more prisoners they take, the less grub they will have for themselves. Like an overzealous prosecuting attorney Dos Passos raises doubts in the jury's mind and brings about the reaction: "The accused can't be all that bad." For instance, after the Armistice, John Andrews wangles an assignment to study music in Paris. On a holiday outing he is picked up as a possible deserter. When he fails to salute the officer who is questioning him, he is knocked down, and without a trial is sent to a forced labor camp. During the whole of his wartime service, Andrews, a Harvard graduate, rails against the "slavery" of the life of a private but so hates the officer class that he will not even try to become a corporal. Thus Dos Passos' valid hatred of war is obscured by his paranoid hatred of everything: officers, YMCA men, clergymen, statesmen, America itself.

Forty-two years later Dos Passos remembered a very different war. In *The Best of Times* (1966) he told of meeting a general who was "an old dear," of Sergeant O'Reilly, who was a "natural leader. . . . The boys enjoyed serving under him." The germ of Private Andrews' disastrous excursion was probably Dos Passos' own experience when as a student in Paris after the Armistice he went AWOL in search of his missing army record. After dodging MP's he reached Tours where "a Top Sergeant, a prince among men" led him through a maze of red tape and produced the missing record. Dos Passos got back to his barracks in time for roll call, and with his record in hand was able to get an honorable discharge.[21]

The distortion of the incident as represented in *Three Soldiers* is all the more unforgivable because the novel is designed to appear as a documentary, almost as reportage. The justification of realistic fiction should be an honest picture of reality. By contrast it would seem that much of *Three Soldiers* is a slanted piece of propaganda. Everything is unpleasant. Andrews says, "France is stifling. . . . It stifles you very slowly, with beautiful silk bands. . . . America beats your brains out with a policeman's billy." And a little later he tells a French boy, "Life is very ugly in America."

This last Dos Passos set out to demonstrate in *Manhattan Transfer*. Almost every character is introduced with a disparaging phrase. The first paragraph sets the tone:

> The nurse holding the basket at arm's length as if it were a bedpan, opened the door to the big hot room with greenish distempered walls where in the air tinctured with the smells of alcohol and iodoform hung writhing a faint sourish squalling from the

baskets along the wall. As she set her basket down she glanced into it with pursued-up lips. The newborn baby squirmed into [sic] its cottonwool feebly like a knot of earthworms.

After opening this can of worms Dos Passos introduced the reader to "a lanternjawed grayfaced" nurse, to "a long-toothed blond woman," to "a man with a bottlenose," to one with "a long cigarnosed face," to "a weazlish man with gold teeth"; to "a bigjawed man with pigeyes"; to a man "with silver hair and a red hawkface"; to "two men with chinless bluefish faces"; to "a hawkbeaked woman with crimson hair"; to "a rawboned man with big sagging eyes like oysters." And so it goes throughout the novel. It is difficult to find in *Manhattan Transfer* any view other than a paranoid hatred of the human race. At the end Jimmy Herf, having given up the newspaper job he detests, takes a symbolic walk out of the city. The truckdriver who gives him a lift asks:

> "How fur ye goin?"
> "I dunno . . . Pretty fur."

Writing in 1929 Edmund Wilson commented on the impact of Dos Passos' plays and novels:

> Now, the life of middle-class America, even under capitalism and even in a city like New York, is not so unattractive as Dos Passos makes it—no human life under any conditions can ever have been so unattractive. Under however an unequal distribution of wealth, human beings are still capable of enjoyment, affection and enthusiasm—even of integrity and courage. . . .

Wilson suggested that the American bathroom and the Ford car may have done more to improve the lives of ordinary people than had the prophets of revolution. Therefore:

> Might it not, we ask ourselves, be possible—have we not, in fact seen it occur—for a writer to hold Dos Passos' political opinions and yet not depict our middle-class republic as a place where no birds sing, no flowers bloom and where the very air is almost unbreathable? For, in the novels and plays of Dos Passos, everybody loses out . . . when so intelligent a man and so good an artist allows his bias so to falsify his picture of life . . . its values are partly those of melodrama—we begin to guess some stubborn sentimentalism at the bottom of the whole thing—some deeply buried streak of hysteria. . . .[22]

As has often happened, the hysteria, the paranoid view of America provided the ground work for the left-wing writing of the next decade. Dos Passos' sense of alienation carried over into his trilogy *U.S.A.* Technically it is far superior to *Manhattan Transfer;* some of the innovations like the "Newsreel" and "Camera Eye" sections brought a new dimension to fiction.

Because *U.S.A.*, especially the second and third novels, belongs to the proletarian school of writing of the 1930s, it falls somewhat beyond the scope of this study. However the first novel, *The 42nd Parallel* (1930), preserves in amber the radicalism of the pre-war period. The heroes presented in the biographical sketches are Eugene V. Debs, Big Bill Haywood, the elder Robert La Follette—"Fighting Bob." In this novel Dos Passos' heart belongs not to the Communists but to the Wobblies. Even in *Nineteen-Nine-*

teen there is a sketch of the I.W.W. bard, Joe Hill. Pervading this novel is the mood of the twenties—its disillusion with World War I. The "Meester Veelson" sketch drips venom.

This second novel also shows a further shift to the left. In the portrait of Paxton Hibben, called "A Hoosier Quixote," there are such comments as

> The talk of social justice petered out; T.R. was a windbag like the rest of 'em, the Bull Moose was stuffed with the same sawdust as the G.O.P.

Then in Paris while "they were still haggling over the price of blood, squabbling over toy flags. . . ."

> In Moscow there was order,
> In Moscow there was work,
> In Moscow there was hope; . . .

As in *Three Soldiers* and *Manhattan Transfer* most of the fictional characters are either corrupt or defeated.

Dos Passos, like Hemingway, belonged to what Gertrude Stein called "the lost generation." It came to mean a generation disoriented by World War I and its aftermath. However as earlier chapters suggest, the mood of disillusion antedates the war. *Spoon River* began to appear in 1914; Lewis conceived *Main Street* as *The Village Virus* as early as 1905; [23] *Winesburg, Ohio* shows no mark of events after 1914; Eliot's *Waste Land* mood appears in the *Prufrock* volume of 1917. In all probability *Prufrock* and *Portrait of a Lady* are the fruits of his pre-war experience in Boston.

Obviously war novels like Dos Passos' *Three Soldiers*, Faulkner's *Soldier's Pay* and Hemingway's *A Farewell to*

Arms are the result of the catastrophe of 1914–1918 and its aftermath. But the emotional roots of Dos Passos' *Manhattan Transfer* and *U.S.A.* are very much in the radical tradition of pre-war America—the era of Bill Haywood and Eugene V. Debs; Faulkner's characteristic world is that of the post-bellum South. The impact of science on traditional beliefs—Krutch's bête noire—goes at least as far back as Tennyson's *In Memoriam* and Arnold's *Dover Beach*.

The real case against the writers of the 1920s is not that one or another of them saw the modern world, and especially the United States, as a wasteland but that so many of them did. This might seem to document their gloomy view of modern society; on the other hand it suggests that the writers and intellectuals took in each other's washing. One is reminded of Daisy's remark in Edmund Wilson's novel *I Thought of Daisy*. When asked where she got the line about the downfall of western civilization, she answered, "Oh that was just something I picked up at the Ritz Bar in Paris."

Some of the wasteland attitude can, like Daisy's, be explained as a response to fashion, but long-held attitudes can become a mental habit. Paranoia is a contagious disease. Certainly it is dangerous in a social critic; he tends to make others see his distorted vision. The very unanimity of the writers of the twenties is an indication that almost none of them was looking at the scene with fresh eyes.

To take a few examples of what Blake called the single vision: for every bored woman in a boudoir or a Daisy Buchanan there were scores of college girls going out with idealism and enthusiasm to take jobs as teachers, scholars, social workers, physicians and lawyers. No society in history had made higher education available to such a large proportion of women. In fact, higher education for women is almost an American invention.

The wasteland women who remember playing at the archduke's, walking in the Hofgarten, or who expect the hot water to be brought at ten are essentially anachronistic; they are representative not of the modern world but of the Edwardian era.

Or take the alleged evils of science and technology which had so disturbed Krutch, Mumford, and the Agrarians. As has been pointed out in Chapter 6 there was a considerable element of paranoia in attacks on the Machine. Biological discoveries which so disturbed Ransom and Krutch had conquered hookworm in the South. Walter Reed and his associates had through the conquest of yellow fever made the Panama Canal possible and had eliminated a scourge which in the nineteenth century devastated cities like Philadelphia and New Orleans. In 1922 Dr. John M. Dodson, Dean of Rush Medical College, stated that in the last half century twelve to fourteen years had been added to the average human life; infant mortality had been cut in half.[24] Great scourges like diphtheria and tuberculosis were rapidly being wiped out.

Freudian psychology proved to be a new tool for the treatment of mental illness. In the Minnesota of Gopher Prairie and Zenith, the Mayo brothers had established a world-famous medical center; in supposedly benighted Kansas the Menningers had begun their great psychiatric hospital.

The argument that such advances are merely a form of improving man's physical comfort is about as sensible as arguing that there was nothing spiritual involved in Christ's healing of the sick. Only if spirituality is equated with wearing a hair shirt and refusing to bathe or with some form of ritualistic observance can one deny the spiritual quality of men dedicated to the conquest of disease. The men who voluntarily subjected themselves to yellow fever are at least as admirable as those who died to defend their interpretation of the eucharist. Limited as his vision often was, Sinclair Lewis in *Arrowsmith* showed an understanding of the selfless dedication of the true scientist.

Edmund Wilson's remarks on Dos Passos might well apply to the picture of America drawn by the writers of the second renaissance: "a place where no birds sing, no flowers bloom, and where the air is almost unbreathable." Certainly their "values are partly those of melodrama . . . we begin to guess some stubborn sentimentalism at the bottom of the whole thing—some deeply buried streak of hysteria . . ."—in other words a paranoid vision.

8.

The Score Card

There are several criteria for evaluating a literary period: its impact on its own time, its legacy to later periods, its creation of enduring works, its achievement in comparison with that of other eras. All of these criteria have been implicit and sometimes explicit in the foregoing chapters. However a summing up of the evidence is in order.

Judged by its impact on its own time, the literary work of the second American renaissance can scarcely be over-estimated. One need only think of the key words and phrases it added to the language: *Main Street, babbitt, the lost generation, the wasteland, the jazz age,* and for a time at least Mencken's *booboisie* and *Bible Belt.* To a lesser degree *Spoon River* and *Winesburg, Ohio* became symbols as well as book titles. It is safe to say that no novel since *Uncle Tom's Cabin* had such a social impact as either *Main Street* or *Babbitt.*

In the 1960s it is difficult to realize the excitement generated forty years earlier by the announcement of a new novel by Lewis, Dreiser, Cabell, Hemingway, Fitzgerald, or by an issue of *The American Mercury*. Harper's announced new volumes of poems by Edna St. Vincent Millay in full-page advertisements resembling invitations to a coronation. A play by O'Neill not only packed the theater but provoked pages of discussion. Less prominent writers like Hergesheimer and Willa Cather were read by intellectuals as well as by subscribers to *The Saturday Evening Post*. The passionate controversies about "the new poetry" or Dreiser, Mencken, and Lewis have perhaps no modern parallel in the field of literature. These writers were the subjects of editorials in both the metropolis and the boondocks. Clergymen preached sermons on, or usually against, current literature.

Today it would seem strange to hear a university professor complaining about the influence of a single magazine as did the one who deplored the ubiquity of *The Mercury* under students' arms. If *Playboy* now occupies that position it is for much the same reasons that students of an earlier day bought *Shadowland* with its near-nudes and *Captain Billy's Whizbang* for its off-color jokes. In the twenties they read *The Mercury* for intellectual stimulation. Some of them read *Poetry, The New Republic, The Nation,* and *The Dial*. Probably at no time since the controversy over slavery had American students up to that time taken so much interest in the ferment of ideas.

This statement may seem strange in view of the flaming-youth aspect of the period, a view immortalized by the stories of Fitzgerald and the drawings of John Held, Jr. But it will be remembered that at Princeton, Amory Blaine somewhat naively began to explore the world of ideas.

Fitzgerald once described *This Side of Paradise* as "a Romance and a reading list." [1] *The Plastic Age* (1924) by Percy Marks also shows students beginning to discuss intellectual matters. This is in marked contrast with the pictures of college students of a generation earlier. Charles Flandrau's *Harvard Episodes,* Owen Wister's *Philosophy 4,* Owen Johnson's *Stover at Yale*—all show a collegiate world almost wholly concerned with clubs, football, eating, and drinking. In *Philosophy 4* a socialist student is scathingly satirized, his hard study is made ridiculous by the cleverness of the wealthy playboys Bertie and Billy. It was the era caricatured in *Old Siwash.*

This is not to say that most college students between 1915 and 1930 participated in an intellectual renaissance any more than one can say that the circulation of *The Saturday Evening Post* suffered because of *The Mercury* and *The Dial.* But the renaissance in higher education was beginning.

There is also substantial evidence that the literary explosion of the period had its greatest influence on women. The War had brought them out of the kitchen and the parlor to work on committees, in offices, and factories. They paraded to publicize the Red Cross and Liberty Bonds. A considerable number went overseas as nurses and volunteers. It is significant that much of the literature of the period reflected a revolution in sexual mores. Under the traditional double standard, Puritanism had laid a much heavier hand on women than on men. Kinsey's findings a generation later indicated that for fifty years the amount of masculine pre-marital experience had remained more or less constant; whereas a variety of studies indicated an increase in pre-marital sex for the girls following World War I. The rather mild form of courtship called spooning was succeeded by much more vigorous petting and necking—activities greatly facilitated by short dresses, bobbed hair, and the discarding of corsets. In women's clubs the discussion of the new and sometimes shocking novels was particularly lively.

The shift in interest from adventure, politics, and economics over to sex and social mores can be illustrated by comparing the stories and novels of Hamlin Garland, Stephen Crane, Jack London, Frank Morris, and Henry B. Fuller with those of Floyd Dell, Sherwood Anderson, Carl Van Vechten, Ben Hecht, James Branch Cabell, and Ellen Glasgow. Dreiser of course dealt with both sex and big business. Lewis is something of an exception to the prevailing trend; in many ways he is closer to the tradition of Garland, Fuller, and Norris, in that love and sex are subordinated to the social criticism. By contrast, although *The Great Gatsby* dealt with the social and political effects of prohibition, Fitzgerald almost completely subordinated this theme to the drama of love and sex.

The sexual element in *The Spoon River Anthology* made it notorious despite the fact that only about 38 of the 244 epitaphs deal primarily with the sexual experience of the characters. On the other hand in Anderson's *Winesburg, Ohio* with its Freudian overtones, the theme of sexual frustration is central, as it is in his *Many Marriages*. As has been noted, much of the attack on the new literature was based upon its alleged sexual immorality. Although Mayor Jimmie Walker once remarked that he never heard of a woman who was seduced by a book, it remains true that a substantial body of poetry, drama, and fiction attacked the Victorian idea of morality and represented sexual experience both inside and outside of marriage as normal and desirable.

Literature was by no means solely responsible for the sexual revolution; in part it merely reflected it. However the teachings of Freud on the effects of sexual repression—teachings often misrepresented—reached the average man through literature rather than from Freud's writings. The effect of World War I on American mores has probably been exaggerated. As the autobiographies of such people as Max Eastman, Hutchins Hapgood, and Mabel Dodge Luhan show, a considerable amount of sexual freedom prevailed in avant garde circles. Dreiser's novels, including the autobiographical *The Genius,* indicate that the Puritanical code was widely disregarded elsewhere. *Spoon River* of course antedates the War, and works of fiction like *Winesburg, Ohio* (1919), *The Moon Calf* (1920), *The Tattooed Countess* (1924), *Desire Under the Elms* (1925) are all laid in pre-war America.

Malcolm Cowley is surely right in saying, "The real war had been fought during the decade before 1920, when almost every new writer was a recruit to the army against gentility, and when older writers like Dreiser and Robinson were being rescued from neglect and praised as leaders." [2] The terrific impact of the writing of the 1920s was largely due to the fact that it was the crest of a wave. For a generation at least the complacencies of middle-class America had been under attack, especially by the muckrakers in popular magazines. As has been argued in Chapter 2 the Puritan tradition was by no means so widely accepted as the rebels claimed. *The Damnation of Theron Ware*—a best seller in 1896—has exposed the narrowness and hypocrisy of evangelical Protestantism. Hamlin Garland, Frank Norris, Henry B. Fuller, Robert Herrick, and of course Dreiser had vividly represented the corruptions of business and politics.

It is true that several major talents emerged in the post-war years, notably Lewis, Hemingway, Fitzgerald, Dos Passos, Faulkner, and Wolfe, although the impact of the last three was felt chiefly after 1930. In poetry it was only after the war that Pound with *Hugh Selwyn Mauberly* and especially Eliot with *The Waste Land* emerged out of the minor leagues. Probably the most important new poetic voice was Stevens with *Harmonium* which contained the superb *Sunday Morning*. But the post-war years also saw the emergence of Cummings, Williams, MacLeish, Hart Crane, and Marianne Moore. And in drama there was the towering figure of O'Neill. All these added to the still producing earlier writers such as Dreiser, Robinson, and Frost created an exciting literary scene. As John W. Aldridge says: "It takes no literary historian to recognize a vintage year in retrospect: in 1925, for instance, Sinclair Lewis published *Arrowsmith;* Dreiser, *An American Tragedy;* Dos Passos, *Manhattan Transfer;* Fitzgerald, *The Great Gatsby;* Faulkner had just finished *Soldier's Pay;* and Hemingway was working on *The Sun Also Rises.*" [3] In fiction Aldridge could have added Hemingway's *In Our Time,* Anderson's *Dark Laughter;* Cather's *The Professor's House,* and Ellen Glasgow's *Barren Ground.* It was also the year of Eliot's *Poems, 1909–25,* Jeffers' *Roan Stallion,* O'Neill's *Desire Under the Elms,* and Williams' *In the American Grain.**

These writers came at a fortunate time. Thirty years of pioneering work had gradually prepared a reading public to accept work outside the genteel tradition. And despite a national desire to return to normalcy and keep cool with Coolidge there was a deep sense of uneasiness—a malice reflected at sub-intellectual levels by the Ku Klux Klan, the American Legion, the red scares, the firing of college professors. The more intellectually aware citizens were prepared to read books which questioned the pieties

---

* It will be remembered that in this work Williams called Americans "a race incapable of flower."

of the past. The comfortable pre-war era had gone, and the great crusade had ended in a chaotic world.

Furthermore, as John W. Aldridge has pointed out, the reigning novelists were still addressing a middlebrow audience. So too were poets such as Frost, Sandburg, Masters, and Millay who were writing about experiences the middlebrow had shared at least vicariously. Very possibly he had grown up in a Spoon River, a Winesburg, or a Gopher Prairie. The newspapers had made him familiar with Sandburg's Chicago. The parties at Gatsby's house were not very different from those at his own country club or those he had at least heard about; he knew that the World Series had been fixed by a man very like Meyer Wolfsheim. Even a Jake Barnes was "there but for the grace of God go I." The reader met George F. Babbitt daily. In Amandus Pickerbaugh he recognized a caricature of his city's director of public health or superintendent of schools. Remembering Billy Sunday and the headlines about Aimee Semple McPherson he found even Elmer Gantry almost believable. The young matron of 1925 had known and perhaps envied girls who burned their candles at both ends.

However there was in this period the beginnings of a literature which did not represent middlebrow ideas and experience. Perhaps the key document here is Eliot's *The Waste Land,* but much of the poetry of Pound, Wallace Stevens, and Marianne Moore appealed chiefly to those with a sophisticated intellectual background, trained to appreciate subtleties of form and structure. Now that this poetry has been made a staple of undergraduate instruction, it is easy to forget that it once seemed incomprehensible to the middlebrow reader. With a literary background of English poetry and novels he was not prepared to cope with a poetry and body of criticism which had roots in Dante, Provencal poetry, the French Symbolists, and even more esoteric sources. Speaking of the impact of *The Waste Land* on American poets, William Carlos Williams wrote:

> It wiped out our world as if an atom bomb had dropped on it and our brave sallies into the unknown were turned to dust. . . .
>   I felt at once it had set me back twenty years and I'm sure it did. Critically Eliot returned us to the classroom. . . .[4]

The middlebrow reader, although interested in poetry, had little desire to be returned to the classroom. The American novelists were somewhat slower in demanding such a return, but the *Ulysses* of James Joyce clearly set up this academic requirement. Joyce once said, "The demand that I make of my reader is that he shall devote his whole life to a reading of my works." [5] To a lesser degree Faulkner presented considerable difficulty to the reasonably literate reader. Aldridge cites him as "the classic modern example, of an important novelist who was discovered and sustained by criticism long before his name was widely known, and who even at that, remained to the end of his life much better known to the general public for his critical reputation than for his books—which were more admired than read." [6]

It will be remembered that the first American publication of *Ulysses* was in *The Little Review*—that is until it was stopped in mid-course by the Post Office Department. Similarly *The Waste Land* first appeared in this country in *The Dial*. In many respects these periodicals symbolized the growing split between the highbrow and the middlebrow audience. *The Little Review* in particular went in for avant-garde writing, including a good bit of dadaist verse. Its editor, Margaret Anderson, called *The Dial* a dealcoholized version of *The Little Review*.[7] In summing up the fifteen years of the magazine's existence Miss Anderson said that it "had given space to 23 new systems of art (all now dead) representing 19 countries."[8] Similarly, expatriate magazines like *Broom* and *Transition* favored avant-garde writing.

But in the second renaissance the split between the highbrow and the middlebrow was by no means absolute. The real war was between generations; the old establishment adhering to the genteel tradition versus the rebels against that tradition. To an astonishing degree the new and experimental writers who were first given a hearing in the little magazines became within a few years acceptable to middlebrow readers. Poets like Masters, Frost, Pound, Sandburg, Eliot, Lindsay, Amy Lowell, and Marianne Moore got their first American publication in magazines of limited circulation: *Reedy's Mirror, Poetry, The Dial.* A number of these poets soon became widely read. Pound and Eliot became well-known if not so widely read. Margaret Anderson claimed to have been the first to publish Hemingway's short stories.[9] In Paris the expatriate presses of Robert McAlmon and Harry Crosby also pioneered in publishing Hemingway. Sherwood Anderson, grateful to *The Little Review* for giving him a hearing, gave it first chance at stories for which he could have received pay in *The Dial*.[10] He also appeared in *The Seven Arts.* By 1919 some of these stories which only highbrow magazines would accept were included in *Winesburg, Ohio,* which became something of a popular success. Scribner's brought out Hemingway's *In Our Time* in 1925 and

The Sun Also Rises in 1926, thus establishing him as a popular writer.

In fact Aldridge's *Time to Murder and Create* (1966) is essentially a lament for the American novel since the 1920s when first-rate writers appealed to both highbrow and middlebrow. Much the same fate has overtaken poetry. The poets of the second renaissance had a much larger public than do those of the 1960s. Thus despite the foreshadowing of a break between the intellectual and the educated reader there was a considerable amount of shared interest in literature. Today an educated person unless he is a part of the literary establishment or a member of an English department, reads little fiction and less poetry once he gets out of college.

When one remembers the slow recognition of Melville, Thoreau, and Whitman as major writers it might seem that the second American renaissance was a golden age. By 1930 most of its major figures were already in the hall of fame. Lewis' Nobel Prize address of that year is a kind of hagiography. In 1940, 1950, or even 1960 many of the same names would appear, but in those thirty years no comparable list could be added.

The writers of those golden years had finally broken the shackles of the genteel tradition; they had created new kinds of poetry; they had transformed the theater from entertainment into a serious forum; they had made literary experimentation not only respectable but mandatory; they had developed a body of literary criticism hitherto unequalled in the United States; and above all they had made literature exciting and controversial, had made it as perhaps never before or since a vital part of the American scene. Why then is their total effort so disappointing? Why was their legacy of so little use to their successors?

The answers to these questions have been suggested in the foregoing chapters. There is some justice in Maxwell Geismar's comment on the period:

> For this entire movement of the American twenties, fresh and promising, varied in talent and bold in achievement, seems to end almost everywhere on a note of negation and exhaustion. Winesburg, Ohio, gave way to New York, and New York to Paris and Capri, and Capri to the Wasteland. This was the last resort, the true home of these innovators and rebels.[11]

Malcolm Cowley spoke of a "feeling of promises unfulfilled and powers never translated into deeds or works." [12] He cited the inferior later work of Dreiser, Lewis, and Cather; the retirement of Brooks from contemporary literature; Sandburg traveling around with a guitar. He could have added the decline of Hemingway after *A Farewell to Arms* and cited the Eliot of *The Cocktail Party* and *The Confidential Clerk*. A significant number of the writers took the escape route of alcohol, among them Lewis, Lardner, Hart Crane, and of course Fitzgerald. Hemingway's highly autobiographical *The Snows of Kilimanjaro* is a kind of confession that high living had blighted his talent. The sense of alienation in the writers of the era was in itself a debilitating force.

Cowley suggested that the rich promise was blighted by the War, the betrayal of the cause by the Socialist leaders, the failure of the hope raised by Wilson's promises, the drive against the radicals, and the complete victory of big business. This explanation is inadequate. As the present study has demonstrated, the notes of negation and defeat had been sounded before the War; and the vintage years came in the 1920s. Certainly the drive against the radicals had little relevance to the work of such writers as Mencken, Eliot, Cather, Hemingway, Fitzgerald, or Faulkner.

Bernard De Voto may be closer to the truth in his theory that the writers were viewing the scene through literature instead of looking at the realities of American life. But one can hardly accuse Dreiser, Lewis, Fitzgerald, and Dos Passos of a bookish view of life. For better or worse they kept their eyes on the American scene. De Voto is of course right in arguing that they failed to see the whole picture, the dynamic side of a society which had created the most powerful nation on earth, which was feeding half the globe, and which even in the Harding-Coolidge era gave more of its citizens freedom and economic opportunity than was enjoyed anywhere else. Until the gates were partially shut by the exclusion act of 1921, thousands of immigrants annually abandoned the old world for the new.

It might even be argued that the basic idealism of Americans was a major cause for the bitter criticism of their own country. Human beings and human institutions always fell short of the utopian vision which had existed since the Declaration of Independence and which characterized our literature from Jefferson to Parrington. Lincoln Steffens discovered that in Europe business and political corruption was so institutionalized as to be an accepted way of life as opposed to the American attack on these evils. It is symbolic that a major difference between a Carol Kennicott and an Emma Bovary is that the American woman tried to improve a dull village; whereas the French woman merely tried to escape one through sexual adventure.

This utopianism is related to the only-in-America fallacy so often mentioned in this study. Just as Shelley, fleeing Regency England, envisioned a Greek isle which preserved a golden age and to which he could flee with Emilia, so American writers pictured happy European peasants and villagers far different from the people of Spoon River and Winesburg. Standardization, which seemed so crass in a Ford car, looked quaint when a European peasant cut grain with a sickle unchanged in design for hundreds of years. In this myopia the American rebels displayed a certain amount of provinciality. Although they had read Ibsen, Shaw, and Wells, they often failed to recognize that these writers had been at war with the same genteel tradition which American writers found so stultifying at home.

The pervasive theme of escape from a stultifying cultural environment to Chicago, New York, or Paris is a reflection of the social mobility possible to Americans. This social and spatial mobility which was remarked on long ago by Franklin and Crèvecoeur and which accounted for the rapid settling of a vast land mass, is obviously related to the utopian dream of finding a better world. In the twentieth century it often took the form of a reverse trek back to the city, the Eastern seaboard, or Europe.

The effect of the rapid social change of the twentieth century, especially the effect of increasing urbanization on mores and values has already been mentioned. However, despite the impressive body of fiction and criticism reflecting the new values, it is difficult to name a single literary work which deals with this phenomenon of social change. Almost without exception the writers rejected the older village and middle-class values, but no one of them revealed that the nation as a whole was revising these values. The huge success of a *Spoon River, Main Street,* or a *What Price Glory* is testimony to a widespread new climate of opinion. Mencken and his cohorts made much of the anti-evolution statute of Tennessee; they had little or nothing to say of the growth of great universities throughout the nation, fine metropolitan museums and symphony orchestras, or the creation of a Mayo Clinic or a Rockefeller Foundation for research.

The cultural wasteland depicted by Brooks, Mencken, Frank, Lewisohn, Lewis, Williams, and others had as early as 1912 begun a revolution in English poetry. With the exception of Yeats there was probably no British twentieth-century poet as important as Frost, Pound, Eliot, Stevens, Cummings, or even Masters and Lindsay—certainly none as original—until the appearance of Auden, Spender, and Mac Neice in the 1930s. The editor of a leading American publishing house remarked that about 1929 his company began to issue more native than foreign work. Obviously a new tide had been running for some years.

As has been pointed out in earlier chapters, important sources of this myopia about the American scene were the literary and academic establishments. Both were dominated by the Jamesean view of our culture. Until the thirties and forties few college alumni had ever had a course in American literature. One English major who graduated from a prominent college in 1923 remembers that by then he had never read anything by Emerson, Thoreau, Melville, James, or Whitman except *Captain My Captain*. On his way to the doctorate he never met any of these in the classroom.

On the other hand there were courses, often required, in American history, in economics, and political science. In these, however, as is indicated by the widespread acceptance of Beard's *An Economic Interpretation of the Constitution*, the point of view was often highly critical of American institutions. One cause for this academic alienation was the changed status of the professor. In college towns of the nineteenth century he had been a respected, often prominent, member of the community. He dined with the local gentry, the banker, the leading businessmen. His moderate salary nevertheless made it possible for him to travel in Europe with his family. It was not unusual for a professor to be a mayor or member of a town council. After World War I all of this changed. Both colleges and communities grew larger: the college town became a city run by a political machine. Most important was the professor's decline in economic status. By 1920 his purchasing power declined to 68.9 percent of the pre-war level. It was not until 1927 that faculty salaries bought as much as they did in 1914. The professor could no longer move in the same circles with bankers and businessmen. As far as he was concerned the American system was faulty and particularly hostile to the intellectual. The growing alienation of the professors from the business community as represented by boards of trustees is reflected in Robert Herrick's novel, *Chimes* (1916), in Veblen's *The Higher Learning in America* (1918) and Sinclair's *The Goose Step* (1923), all of which deal with suppression of academic freedom.

The limitations of the academic world help to explain but do not justify the myopia of so much of the intellectual community. It is not, as MacLeish charged, that they were irresponsible; instead throughout the whole period there is a note of passionate conviction. They wanted nothing less than to make over the United States. But like the highway planners and redevelopment enthusiasts of the 1960s, the intellectuals of the second renaissance were too ready to destroy everything hitherto standing. The occupational hazard of the intellectual is to subordinate everything to some single utopian purpose; he is disturbed by the untidy and the nonrational inheritances from the past. This is nowhere more evident than in the already cited willingness of both the leftists and the conservatives to jettison the humane values of the liberal tradition. It is also evident in the attempt to reduce romantic love to a biological function and to equate family relationships to Oedipus complexes.

The same tendency appears in the rejection of middle-class values, especially as reflected in small-town life. Certainly the American small town, like villages everywhere, had mean and narrow characteristics, but it was surely not the joyless place depicted by the intellectuals. The singing around the piano, the dancing to the Victrola, the church "sociables," the ball games, the family picnics and young peoples' doggie roasts, the men's hunting and fishing provided a kind of relaxed enjoyment of life. Men and women worked hard but at a less driving pace than was customary in the city. Sentimentalized as it was, Thornton Wilder's *Our Town* (1938) is at least as true as *Main Street*. Fitzgerald understood something of this when he had Nick Carraway say:

> That's my Middle West—not the wheat or the prairies or the lost Swede towns but the thrilling returning trains of my youth, and the street lamps and sleigh bells in the frosty dark, and the shadows of holly wreaths thrown by lighted windows on the snow. I am part of that, a little solemn with the feel of those long winters, a little complacent from growing up in the Carraway house in a city where dwellings are still called through decades by a family's name.

To an extent matched nowhere in the world the middle-class people of the Gopher Prairies and Zeniths sent their boys and girls to college. There was an economic motive of course, as there always is in the preparation for a career. But it is surely no accident that so many of the intellectuals of the second renaissance traveled the road from a village or provincial city to college and then to literature: Pound, Eliot, Lewis, Cather, Fitzgerald, Stevens, Williams, Hart Crane, Tate, Faulkner—to mention only a few. Obviously there must have been some seedbed of intellectual culture, some respect for the things of the mind and spirit. In fact the literary flowering of the period is the best refutation of the oft repeated charge that America was a cultural wasteland. No renaissance springs up *de novo;* it is always the product of a culture.

It was the failure to recognize the vigor of our native culture which was a major defect of the writers between 1910 and 1930. As has been argued, there was an adolescent quality in the revolt, a rebellion against one's father. In the late 1930s and early 1940s writers like Brooks and MacLeish began, like Mark Twain, to discover how much the old man had learned in a few years.

An even greater failure of the intellectuals of the era was surely in the field of politics. The moribund or mountebank democracy which they portrayed managed to survive a great economic crisis without becoming a totalitarian Communist or Fascist state; it successfully fought a global war. The prophets of the left were wrong in predicting the collapse of capitalist society and a dictatorship of the proletariat; those of the right were equally wrong in their argument that American society was so flabby and undisciplined that it needed some kind of autocratic rule.

This whoring after strange gods came to its logical conclusion in the 1930s, which Auden called "a low dishonest decade." MacLeish and De Voto are surely right in attributing much of the unedifying spectacle to the teachings of the second renaissance. Like the one from 1840 to 1855 it determined a climate of opinion and standards of value.

One great difference between the two periods was that the first was essentially positive, the second negative. Emerson, Thoreau, and Whitman had used the ideals of the Puritans and the founding fathers as the basis for a sometimes utopian vision of the future of the nation. The writers of the later renaissance denied the value of this heritage and ended with an essentially nihilistic view of the United States. The rebuilding of American political institutions after 1932 followed the directions pointed out by Jefferson, Jackson, and Lincoln, not by the Marxists or the New Humanists. The revolution in higher education was built upon the foundations laid by Emerson and Thoreau. Emerson had called for an understanding of contemporary culture; both men had argued for what is essentially the experimental method as opposed to rote learning. Emerson would have staffed the ideal college with such men as Allston, Greenough, Webster, and Carlyle.

In a later period John Dewey, an heir to Emersonian doctrines, nevertheless sowed the seeds of an anti-intellectualism that debilitated education until the advent of the first Sputnik. As Admiral Hyman Rickover summed it up, the effect of Dewey's theories "has led to the substitution of know-how subjects for solid learning and to the widespread tendency of schools to instruct pupils in the minutae of daily life. . . ." [13] Emerson had defined the scholar as man thinking; Dewey tended to turn the pupil into child doing.

Another way of evaluating the literature of a period is to consider the enduring quality of its finest works. In his discussion of the American novel, John W. Aldbridge is certainly too sweeping in saying that "Gatsby is one of the very few books left from the twenties that we are still able to read with any kind of enduring pleasure." Certainly one would have to include *Winesburg, Ohio* (although its date is 1919), *The Sun Also Rises* and *A Farewell to Arms* and possibly to *The Sound and the Fury* and *Look Homeward, Angel.* And in any discussion of the movers and shakers of the period it is easy to forget such good novels as Wharton's *Age of Innocence,* Glasgow's *Barren Ground* and *The Romantic Comedians,* Hergesheimer's *Java Head.* However, although these reflect the sensibility of the twenties they are essentially re-creations of the past.

It is ironic that the rebels who were so contemptuous of America's literary past created few novels of the stature of *The Scarlet Letter, Moby Dick, Billy Budd, Huckleberry Finn, Daisy Miller, Portrait of a Lady, The American, The Ambassadors, The Wings of the Dove,* and *The Golden Bowl.* Even a partial list of the novels and stories of Henry James indicates how much more impressive was his achievement than that of many of the later novelists. In fact today Lewis is almost unreadable and Dreiser only somewhat less so.

One reason for this is that James probed more deeply into the psyche: Isabel Archer, Christopher Newman, Lambert Strether, Milly Theale, Maggie Verver are more complex characters than Carrie Meeber, Frank Cowperwood, Clyde Griffiths, Carol Kennicott, or George Babbitt. Sam Dodsworth is a cruder reworking of Christopher Newman. As Philip Young pointed out Hemingway tended to draw a single male character—a projection of himself. The people in Dos Passos' novels tend to merge into a kind of montage.

In poetry it might be a moot question whether Eliot is greater than Walt Whitman, but as Pound said of Whitman, "it was you who broke the new ground." As is well known, Eliot's technique in *The Waste Land* owes much to Pound. One need not agree with Richard Aldington who said of Eliot, "what is original in his poetry is not good, and what is good is not original," [14] but it is doubtful that such an Alexandrian technique is a step forward.

Certainly Whitman and Emily Dickinson can stand comparison with such major twentieth-century figures as Eliot, Frost, and Stevens. And not all critics would agree that Frost is a major poet. However it is possibly true that the first third of this century was richer in poetic achievement than any comparable period in American literature. It may well be that the poetry of the era will be more enduring than the prose. Often the poetry touches deeper levels of feeling, and at its best, like that of Whitman and Dickinson it explores fundamental questions.

So too did the prose of Emerson, Thoreau, Hawthorne, and Melville. It is this very concern with fundamental questions which has made Thoreau a revolutionary force in this century—the teacher of Ghandi and Martin Luther King. Today there are Thoreau societies in France and England and two in Japan.[15] Hawthorne's stories and Melville's *Moby Dick* explore the nature of evil: is it inherent in the creation or is it a human creation? *Billy Budd* dramatizes the ever-recurring problem of law versus justice. The questions with which the nineteenth-century writers dealt are those with which we are concerned and with which our grandchildren will be concerned after us.

By contrast, many of the preoccupations of the twentieth-century prose writers discussed in this study—

including the novelists—such matters as puritanical views of sex, Prohibition, the exploitation of labor, the New Humanism, Agrarianism, the alleged cultural desert—are all hopelessly dated.

Several exceptions come to mind; * Hemingway with his stoic creed for dealing with a meaningless universe; Krutch with a somewhat similar response; Stevens with his aesthetic acceptance of life and death; O'Neill with his sense of man's tragic fate; and Eliot with his concern with spiritual sterility.

As has been suggested earlier, Hemingway's nihilism at times verged on the melodramatic and his "grace under pressure" too often became a tough-guy prose. The creed of the bullfighter and the hunter is inadequate for the complex modern world.

In Krutch's world even the physical and aesthetic satisfactions are absent. As has been argued he gave a paranoid picture of the discomforts of contemporary life, a paranoia verging on melodrama.

In Stevens' world the musing woman finds that "Death is the mother of beauty," and that

> Divinity must live within herself;
> Passions of rain or moods in falling snow;
> Grievings in loneliness, or unsubdued
> Elations when the forest blooms; gusty
> Emotions on wet roads on autumn nights;
> All pleasures and all pains, remembering
> The bough of summer and the winter branch.
> These are the measures destined for her soul.

---

* Possibly one might include Robinson with his theme of man's essential loneliness, and Frost with his portrayal—often simplistic—of certain enduring elements in the psyche.

Seldom has the aesthetic creed found finer expression. This world where "Deer walk upon our mountains, and the quail/Whistle about us their spontaneous cries," is all very lovely, but it lacks the terror of Melville's shark-filled sea; or the brutality of the world Hemingway had experienced in a war where soldiers casually pot Germans as they come over a garden wall; or the psychic turmoil of Faulkner's characters which leads to their self-destruction. An exclusively tragic view of life can omit the basic human aesthetic and sensuous satisfactions, but one which deals only with these satisfactions is incomplete. Stevens leaves small room for tragedy.

On the other hand, O'Neill at his best as in *Desire under the Elms* or *Mourning Becomes Electra* was dealing with the great themes of Aeschylus and Sophocles. But like so much of the work of the twenties O'Neill's work as a whole leaves the impression of negation and defeat. In a way the nihilism of *The Iceman Cometh* (1939) and *A Long Day's Journey into Night* (1956) is the logical conclusion to his earlier work. Nevertheless, as Krutch has pointed out, O'Neill did deal with two great questions: "the question of human responsibility for what is called Fate and the question of what general truth the tragic situation illustrates . . . perhaps the questions which true tragedy always raises." [16]

The limitations of Eliot lie not in the questions he asked but in his evidence and his answers. As has been discussed earlier, Eliot, like so many of his contemporaries, glamorized the past and gave a one-sided picture of modern life. Granting his premise that modern society is spiritually sterile his plea for a return to medieval theology was an inadequate solution to the dilemmas created by historical scholarship and modern science. The theology to which he returned was based on a cosmology and a social order neither of which was relevant to the modern world. In *Ash Wednesday* and *The Journey of the Magi* this theology is implied rather than stated, but in his prose works, especially *The Idea of a Christian Society* (1940) Eliot called for an authoritarian state church embracing most of society. As has been noted, "a spirit of excessive tolerance is to be deplored." This is strikingly similar to Fascist and Communist ideology.

Here again a comparison with Whitman is revealing. *The Journey of the Magi* is based upon a literal acceptance of the story of the birth and crucifixion of the God-man. Whitman dealt with the crucifixion in contemporary terms. In *A Sight in Camp in The Daybreak Gray and Dim* he told of finding three dead soldiers behind the hospital tent. Possibly he intended to suggest the trinity or the three crucifixions; in any case when he lifted the blanket from one figure he found

> a face nor child nor old, very calm, as of
> beautiful yellow-white ivory;
> Young men I think I know you—I think this face
> is the face of Christ himself,
> Dead and divine and brother of us all, and here
> again he lies.

For Eliot the crucifixion took place once long ago; for Whitman it was an ever recurring tragedy. Eliot's vision led him to seek an authoritarian theology; Whitman's raised questions about war and man's inhumanity to man.

The foregoing comparisons between nineteenth-century American literature and that between 1910 and 1930 support the view implicit in this study that despite its immense vitality, the second renaissance was intellectually shallow. This shallowness appears in the misreading of the American past, in the considerable misrepresentation of the contemporary scene, in the failure to recognize the basic values of our society, and in the failure to deal adequately with fundamental questions. Too often it was a literature of ephemeral surfaces. Taken as a whole it lacks breadth of social and philosophical vision.

Notes

INTRODUCTION

1. Robert E. Brown, *Charles Beard and the Constitution, A Critical Analysis* (Princeton, 1955), p. 9.
2. "The Prelude," XI, pp. 294–97.
3. *After the Genteel Tradition: American Writers Since 1910* (New York, 1937), p. 22.
4. Oscar Cargill, *Intellectual America* (New York, 1941), p. 482.
5. *A Book of Prefaces* (New York, 1917), p. 103.

CHAPTER 1

1. Henry James, *William Story and His Friends* (London, 1903), I, 297–98.
2. *A Short History of Painting in America* (New York, 1963), pp. 109–10.
3. *The Wine of the Puritans: A Study of Present-Day America* (London, 1908), p. 136.
4. *The Days of the Phoenix* (New York, 1957), p. 105.
5. *Wine*, p. 15.
6. *Ibid.*, p. 105.
7. *America's Coming of Age* (New York: Anchor, 1958), pp. 63–64.
8. "The Critics and Young America" in *Criticism in America* (New York, 1924), 122.
9. *Letters and Leadership*, reprinted with *America's Coming of Age*, p. 151.

10. *Our America* (New York, 1919), p. 9.
11. *Prefaces,* p. 216.
12. "The Psychoanalytic Insight of Nathaniel Hawthorne," *Psychoanalytic Review,* XXIX (1942), 373–85.
13. *Our America,* p. 70.
14. *Expression in America,* p. 430.
15. *The Seven Arts,* I (November, 1917), 382–83.
16. *A Literary History of America* (1900), p. 335.
17. *Ibid.,* p. 473.
18. Helen Howe, *The Gentle Americans* (New York, 1965), p. 200.
19. *The Days of the Phoenix* (New York, 1957), p. 163.
20. *Exile's Return,* pp. 94–95.
21. *The Theory of American Literature* (Ithaca, 1963), p. 161.
22. *Phoenix,* p. 163.
23. *Intellectual Vagabondage* (New York, 1926), p. 115.
24. *The Ordeal of Mark Twain* (New York, 1920), p. 89.
25. *Ibid.,* p. 324.
26. *Ibid.,* p. 90.
27. *Ibid.,* p. 270.
28. *Ibid.,* p. 250.
29. *Mr. Clemens and Mark Twain* (New York, 1966), p. 161.
30. *Ibid.,* p. 161.
31. *The Nation,* Vol. III, No. 189 (August 14, 1920).
32. *On Native Grounds,* revised (New York, 1956), p. 211.

CHAPTER 2

1. *Wine of the Puritans,* p. 17.
2. *Ibid.,* pp. 19–20.
3. *Letters and Leadership,* p. 140.
4. *Letters of Sherwood Anderson,* ed. by Howard Mumford Jones and Walter B. Rideout (Boston, 1953), p. 59.
5. *The Seven Arts* (April, 1917), p. 633.
6. *Ibid.,* p. 637.
7. *Our America,* p. 149.
8. *Ibid.,* p. 160.
9. *Ibid.,* p. 167.
10. *Prefaces,* pp. 198–99.
11. Louise Collier Willcox, "Thomas Hardy," *North American Review* (March, 1915), p. 425.
12. *In the American Grain* (New York, 1925), p. 68.
13. Florence Emily Hardy, *The Later Years of Thomas Hardy, 1892–1928* (London, 1930), p. 39.
14. Richard Aldington, *Life for Life's Sake* (New York, 1961), p. 229.

15. Frank Luther Mott, *The Golden Multitudes, The Story of Best Sellers in the United States* (New York, 1947).
16. Cargill, p. 415.
17. *Cavalcade of the American Novel* (New York, 1952), p. 313.
18. LHUS, II, 1022.
19. John Macy, *The Spirit of American Literature*, p. 11.
20. "Our Monthly Gossip," *Lippincott's Magazine*, XXXVII (January–June, 1886), 108–109.
21. "Editor's Easy Chair," *Harper's Magazine*, CXXVII, No. DCCLIV (March, 1913), 635.
22. "Editor's Easy Chair," *Harper's Magazine*, CXXVII (August, 1913).
23. *New Republic* (June 19, 1915), pp. 160–61.
24. *New Republic* (September 18, 1915), p. 164.
25. *New Republic* (June 15, 1915), pp. 122–23.
26. *New Republic* (July 31, 1915), p. 335.
27. *New Republic* (September 18, 1915), p. 164.
28. *New Republic* (November, 1915), p. 5.
29. Ellen Duvall, "The New Paganism," *The Atlantic Monthly*, CXXXVI, No. 5 (November, 1925), 635.
30. Daniel Aaron, *P. E. More's Shelburne Essays on American Literature* (New York, 1963), p. 28.
31. *After the Genteel Tradition*, p. 11.
32. *Prejudices*, first series (New York, 1919), p. 11.
33. Stuart Sherman, *Points of View* (New York, 1924), p. 169.
34. *Ibid.*, p. 181.
35. *Prejudices*, first series, p. 88.
36. *Ibid.*, p. 19.
37. *Prefaces*, p. 219.
38. *The American Mercury*, II, No. 7, 255.
39. Cargill, quoted, p. 495.
40. Carl Van Doren, *James Branch Cabell* (New York, 1933, originally 1925), p. 4.
41. *Ibid.*, p. 44.
42. *Ibid.*, pp. 83–84.
43. Cargill, quoted, p. 495.
44. Stern and Gross, quoted, *Ameircan Literary Survey*, p. 124.
45. Kazin, p. 67.
46. *Prefaces*, pp. 106–107.
47. *Ibid.*, p. 138.
48. *Ibid.*, p. 201.
49. "The Dreiser Bugaboo," *The Seven Arts*, II (August, 1917), p. 508.

50. Kaplan, p. 269.
51. *Prefaces*, p. 144.
52. *The Drama Since 1918,* revised ed. (New York, 1965), p. 38.
53. *Ibid.,* p. 50.
54. Wendell, p. 106.
55. Kaplan, p. 274.
56. *Ibid.,* p. 274.
57. *Ibid.,* p. 240.
58. *Ibid.,* p. 263.
59. "An American Humanist," *The Dial* (August 30, 1917), pp. 148–49.
60. *Letters of Theodore Dreiser,* ed. by Robert H. Elias (Philadelphia, 1959), pp. 55–56.
61. Irving Babbitt, *Democracy and Leadership* (Cambridge, 1924).
62. "Putting Down Sin," *The American Mercury,* II, No. 7, 315.
63. *Letters of Sherwood Anderson,* pp. 60–62.
64. *A Story Teller's Story* (New York, 1924), p. 101.
65. *The Drama Since 1918,* p. 16.

CHAPTER 3

1. Daniel Aaron, *P. E. More's Shelburne Essays on American Literature* (New York, 1963), p. 137.
2. Malcolm Cowley, quoted, *"The Critique of Humanism,"* ed. by Hartley Grattan (New York, 1930), pp. 77–78.
3. Aaron, *More's Essays,* p. 21.
4. *Ibid.,* p. 21.
5. Williams, p. 116.
6. *More's Essays,* p. 41.
7. *Ibid.,* p. 44.
8. *American Poetry and Prose,* fourth edition, Part One (Boston, 1957), p. 9.
9. "Criticism," *Selected Essays* (New York, 1935), reprinted, Benet and Pearson, *The Oxford Anthology of American Literature* (New York, 1941), p. 1095.
10. "The Religion of the Day . . . ," *The Emotional Discovery of America* (New York, 1932), pp. 51–52.
11. *Points of View* (New York, 1924), p. 9.
12. *Ibid.,* p. 10.
13. Arthur Schlesinger, Jr., *The Age of Jackson* (Boston, 1945), pp. 369–70.
14. Frederick J. Hoffman, quoted, *The Twenties,* revised ed. (New York, 1962), p. 171n.

15. Edmund Wilson, quoted, "Notes on Babbitt and More," Grattan, p. 44.
16. *Ibid.*, p. 47.
17. Kazin, p. 232.
18. *Democracy and Leadership*, p. 252.
19. *Ibid.*, p. 26.
20. *Ibid.*, p. 261.
21. *Ibid.*, p. 214.
22. *Prefaces*, p. 210.
23. *Prejudices*, II, 46–47.
24. *Ibid.*, p. 137.
25. *Ibid.*, p. 145.
26. *Ibid.*, pp. 47–48.
27. Van Doren, *Cabell*, p. 46.
28. *After the Genteel Tradition*, quoted, p. 106.
29. James Branch Cabell, "Joseph Hergesheimer," *The Bookman*, L, Nos. 3–4 (November–December, 1919) , 273.
30. *Prejudices*, II, 304.
31. *Democracy and Leadership*, p. 240.
32. Hoffman, p. 109.
33. *Prejudices*, II, 201–202.
34. Quoted by Malcolm Cowley in Grattan, pp. 72–73.
35. Kazin, p. 155.
36. *Ibid.*, p. 157.
37. *Points of View*, p. 191.
38. *Expression in America*, p. 269.
39. *Prejudices*, II.
40. Grattan, p. 73.
41. *Prejudices*, II, 47.
42. *Ibid.*, II, 44.
43. *Ibid.*, II, 44.
44. *Ibid.*, II, 42.
45. *Days of the Phoenix*, p. 3.
46. "Tradition and the Individual Talent" from *The Sacred Wood*, reprint (London, 1964), p. 53.
47. "Religion and Literature," *Essays Ancient and Modern* (London, 1936), p. 92; From a talk given in 1934.
48. "An artistic failure," Frye, p. 19.
49. Hoffman, quoted, p. 170n.
50. *Humanism in America* (New York, 1930), pp. 199–202.
51. *Ibid.*, p. 234.
52. *Ibid.*, p. 255.
53. Review of *Arrowsmith*, *The Dial*, LXXVIII (June 1925), 515.

CHAPTER 4

1. *Political Ideas of the Muckrakers* (New York, 1964), pp. 110–111.
2. *Ibid.,* pp. 94–95.
3. *Ibid.,* p. 91.
4. "Playboy Interview with Norman Thomas," *Playboy* (Nov. 1966), p. 96.
5. Robert E. Brown, *Charles Beard and the Constitution* (Princeton, 1956), pp. 8–9.
6. Merle Curti, Richard H. Shyrock, Thomas C. Cochran, and Fred Harvey Harrington, *An American History,* I (New York, 1950), 192, 194.
7. *An Economic Interpretation of the Constitution of the United States* (New York, 1925), p. 17.
8. *Ibid.,* p. 251.
9. *Ibid.,* p. 24.
10. Brown, pp. 38–39.
11. Beard, p. 24.
12. Brown, p. 49.
13. *Ibid.,* p. 20.
14. Beard, p. 45.
15. Brown, p. 55.
15a. *Main Currents in American Thought,* I (New York, 1930), 275.
16. *Ibid.,* I, 355.
17. *Where We Came Out* (New York, 1954), p. 23.
18. *Our America,* p. 14.
19. *The Rediscovery of America* (New York, 1929), p. 149.
20. *In Fear and Trembling* (New York, 1932), p. 181.
21. *Ibid.,* p. 188.
22. *The Little Review,* Vol. I, No. 3 (May 1914).
23. *The Little Review,* Vol. II, No. 1 (Mar. 1916).
24. *The Little Review,* Vol. I, No. 8 (Nov. 1916).
25. *The Little Review,* Vol. III, No. 1 (Mar. 1916).
26. Kazin, p. 136.
27. *The Autobiography of Lincoln Steffens* (New York, 1931), pp. 653–55.
28. *Ibid.,* pp. 656–57.
29. *Looking at Life* (New York, 1924), p. 69.
30. Rod W. Horton and Herbert W. Edwards, *Backgrounds of American Literary Thought* (New York, 1967), p. 230.
31. "Revolutionary Progress," *The Masses* (Feb. 1917), p. 24.
32. *Intellectual Vagabondage* (New York, 1926), p. 148.
33. "Railroads and Revolution," *The Masses* (Nov. 1916).

34. *Intellectual Vagabondage,* p. 154.
35. *Ibid.,* p. 159.
36. Mark Sullivan, *Our Times,* III (New York, 1930), 431.
37. *Our Times,* VI (New York, 1935), 219–20.
38. *The Masses,* IX, No. 10 (Aug. 1917).
39. *Writers on the Left* (New York, 1961), p. 144.
40. *Ibid.,* pp. 120–21.
41. *Ibid.,* quoted, p. 128.
42. "An Apology for Fascism," *The New Republic,* XLIX, No. 632 (Jan. 12, 1927), 213.
43. *Ibid.,* p. 209.
44. *Ibid.,* p. 207.
45. *Where We Came Out,* p. 7.
46. *Ibid,* p. 9.
47. *The New York Times,* Oct. 9, 1917, p. 183.
48. *Notes on Democracy* (New York, 1926), p. 98.
49. *Ibid.,* pp. 59–60.
50. *Ibid.,* p. 48.
51. *Ibid.,* p. 144.
52. *Ibid.,* p. 129.
53. *Ibid.,* p. 150.
54. *The Nation* (Dec. 8, 1926).
55. *The Saturday Review of Literature* (Dec. 11, 1926).
56. Hoffman, quoted, pp. 344 and 345n.
57. Aaron, *More's Essays,* p. 44.
58. *Democracy and Leadership,* p. 207.
59. *Ibid.,* p. 312.
60. *The Letters of Ezra Pound,* ed. by D. D. Paige (New York, 1950), p. 205.
61. Charles Norman, *Ezra Pound* (New York, 1960), p. 392.
62. *Ibid.,* p. 393.
63. Northrop Frye, quoted, p. 11.
64. F. O. Mathiessen, *LHUS,* II (New York, 1948), 1356.
65. *The Criterion,* VIII (July 1929), *Writers,* quoted Aaron, p. 248.
66. Norman, quoted, pp. 174–75.
67. Norman, p. 177.
68. "Blazing Publicity," reprinted in *Vanity Fair,* ed. by Cleveland Amory and Frederick Brodlee (New York, 1960), p. 122.
69. Reprinted in *The Essential Lippmann,* ed. by Clinton Rossiter and James Lare (New York, 1963), p. 114.
70. *Ibid.,* p. 116.
71. Alexander Karanikas, quoted, *Tillers of a Myth, Southern Agrarians as Social and Literary Critics* (Madison, 1966), p. 38.

72. *Ibid.*, quoted, p. 90.
73. *The Growth of the American Republic*, II (New York, 1950), 476.
74. *Ibid.*, II, 477.
75. *Our Times*, VI, 172.
76. Max Eastman, *Love and Revolution* (New York, 1964), pp. 34–35.
77. *Ibid.*, pp. 136–37.
78. *The Masses* (June 1917), p. 22.
79. *Reflections on the Failure of Socialism* (New York, 1955), pp. 50–51.
80. Katherine Drinker Bowen, *Miracle at Philadelphia* (Boston, 1966), p. 14.
81. "When the Big Four Met," *The New Republic* (Dec. 24, 1919); reprinted in *The Faces of Five Decades*, p. 53.

CHAPTER 5

1. *The American Mercury*, I, No. 1 (Jan. 1924), 77.
2. *The American Mercury*, II (May to Aug. 1924), 184.
3. *The American Mercury*, Vol. I.
4. "Genesis or the First Book of the Bible," *Instigations* (New York, 1920), pp. 172–74.
5. *Ibid.*, p. 177.
6. *My Thirty Years War* (New York, 1930), p. 244.
7. *Notes on Democracy*, p. 66.
8. "Sinclair Lewis," reprinted in *Sinclair Lewis, a Collection of Critical Essays*, ed. by Mark Schorer (New York, 1962), p. 91.
9. *Our Times*, VI, 413.
10. Grace Hegger Lewis, *With Love from Gracie* (New York, 1955), p. 187.
11. *The Little Review*, I, No. 4 (June 1914), 1.
12. *Intellectual Vagabondage*, pp. 260–61.
13. Cargill, p. 307.
14. See Richard Kennedy, *The Window of Memory* (Chapel Hill, 1962), pp. 113–217.
15. Carlos Baker, *Ernest Hemingway, A Life Story* (New York, 1969), p. 456.
16. Carlos Baker, *Hemingway the Writer as Artist* (Princeton, 1956), pp. 94–116.
17. Kazin, p. 257.
18. "The Hero and the Code," *Critical Approaches to American Literature*, ed. by Ray B. Browne and Martin Light (New York, 1965), p. 282.

CHAPTER 6

1. *The Critique of Humanism,* ed. by O. Hartley Grattan (New York, 1930), pp. 22–23.
2. Malcolm Cowley, "Humanizing Society," Grattan, p. 75.
3. Karanikas, p. 36.
4. Leo Marx, *The Machine in the Garden* (New York, 1964), p. 8.
5. *The Golden Day* (New York, 1926), p. 120.
6. *Ibid.,* pp. 113–14.
7. Frank, *Rediscovery,* p. 110.
8. John L. Stewart, *The Burden of Time* (Princeton, 1965), p. 110.
9. *Ibid.,* quoted, p. 131.
10. *Ibid.,* p. 158.
11. "Stonewall Jackson, the Good Soldier," quoted, Stewart (New York, 1928), pp. 39–40.
12. *Notes on Virginia* (Richmond, 1853), p. 175.
13. John Crowe Ransom, *God Without Thunder* (New York, 1930), p. 144.
14. *Ibid.,* p. 192.
15. *Ibid.,* pp. 126–27.
16. *Ibid.,* p. 129.
17. *Ibid.,* p. 187.
18. *Ibid.,* p. 187.
19. *The Instinct of Workmanship,* reprint (New York, 1964), pp. 300–301.
20. *Ibid.,* p. 317.
21. *Ibid.,* p. 316.
22. *Technics and Civilization* (New York, 1934), p. 282.
23. Roger Burlingame, *March of the Machines, A Social History of Union through Invention* (New York, 1938), p. 233.
24. Martin R. Cooper, Glen T. Barton, and Albert P. Brodell, *Progress of Farm Mechanization,* U. S. Dept. of Agriculture Miscellaneous Publication, No. 630.
25. *Technics,* p. 274.
26. *Ibid.,* p. 277.
27. *Ibid.,* p. 272.
28. *Ibid.,* p. 313.

CHAPTER 7

1. Kazin, p. 154.
2. *Civilization in the United States, An Inquiry by Thirty Americans* (New York, 1922), p. 141.
3. *Ibid.,* p. 147.
4. *Ibid.,* p. 39.

5. *Ibid.*, p. 98.

6. *Ibid.*, p. 504.

7. Harriet Monroe, *A Poet's Life* (New York, 1938), p. 368.

8. *The Seven Arts*, II (1916–17), 282–83.

9. *America's Coming of Age* (New York, 1958), pp. 98–99.

10. In an interview for the *Paris Review* (1959), quoted William Wasserstrom, "T. S. Eliot and the Dial," *The Sewanee Review*, Vol. LXX, No. 1 (Winter 1962).

11. "The Death of Literary Judgment" from *In Defense of Ignorance* (New York, 1960), reprinted in *Storm over the Wasteland*, ed. by Robert E. Knoll (New York, 1964), p. 150.

12. Hoffman, p. 275.

13. *The Modern Temper* (New York, 1929), pp. 119–20.

14. *Ibid.*, p. 194.

15. *Ibid.*, p. 247.

16. Matthiessen, quoted, II, *LHUS*, 1348.

17. *Ibid.*, p. 1349.

18. Kazin, p. 354.

19. *Ibid.*, p. 356.

20. Edward Wagenknecht, quoted, *Cavalcade of the American Novel* (New York, 1952), p. 421.

21. *The Best of Times* (New York, 1966), p. 78.

22. "John Dos Passos and the Social Revolution" (1929), in *The Shores of Light* (New York, 1952), pp. 432–33.

23. Grace Hegger Lewis, *With Love from Gracie* (New York, 1955), p. 118.

24. *Our Times*, VI, 587.

Chapter 8

1. John W. Aldbridge, *Time to Murder and Create* (New York, 1966), p. 12.

2. *After the Genteel Tradition* (New York, 1937), p. 22.

3. Aldbridge, p. 69.

4. *The Autobiography of William Carlos Williams* (New York, 1951), p. 176.

5. Max Eastman, quoted, *Love and Revolution* (New York, 1964), p. 521.

6. Aldridge, p. 60.

7. *My Thirty Years' War*, p. 189.

8. *Ibid.*, p. 273.

9. *Ibid.*, p. 258.

10. *Ibid.*, p. 44.

11. "A Cycle of Fiction," II, *LHUS*, 1306.
12. *After the Genteel Tradition,* p. 232.
13. *Education and Freedom* (New York, 1959), p. 134.
14. *Ezra Pound and T. S. Eliot* (London, 1954), p. 17.
15. *Realities,* No. 200 (July 1967), 7.
16. Joseph Wood Krutch, *The Drama Since 1918* originally 1939 (New York, 1965), p. 336.

Index